GRADE 7

CORE SKILLS

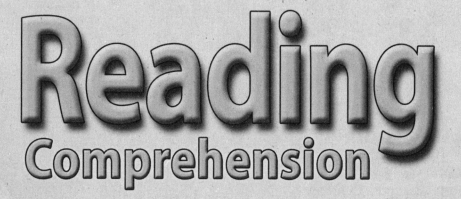

Reading
Comprehension

Harcourt Achieve

Rigby • Steck-Vaughn

www.HarcourtAchieve.com
1.800.531.5015

About the Editor

Donna Loughran is an editor, writer, artist, and multimedia designer living and working in Austin, Texas. She has a B.F.A. in Fine Art and a B.A. in English. She has worked in educational publishing for twelve years.

Acknowledgments

Designer: Julia Hagaman
Cover Design: Alexandra Corona
Interior Illustrations: Donna Loughran
Photography: Donna Loughran, James Freedman

ISBN 978-0-7398-7038-9   ISBN 0-7398-7038-6

Dear Parent,

Welcome to the *Steck-Vaughn Core Skills: Reading Comprehension* series! You have selected a unique book that focuses on developing your child's comprehension skills, the reading and thinking processes associated with the printed word. Because this series was designed with the national standards as a guide, your child will have reading success as well as gain a firm understanding of necessary critical thinking skills.

Reading should be a fun, relaxed activity for children. They should read stories that relate to or build on their own experiences. Vocabulary should be presented in a sequential and logical progression. The stories in this series build on these philosophies to insure your child's reading success. Other important features in this series that will further aid your child include:

- Interesting short reading selections appealing to adolescent readers.

- Vocabulary introduced in context and repeated often.

- Comprehension skills applied in context to make the reading more relevant.

- Multiple choice exercises that develop skills for standardized test taking.

You may wish to have your child read the selections silently or orally, but you will find that sharing the stories and activities with your child will provide additional confidence and support to succeed. When learners experience success, learning becomes a continuous process moving them onward to higher achievements. Moreover, the more your child reads, the more proficient she or he will become.

Enjoy this special time with your child!

Sincerely,
The Educators and Staff of
Steck-Vaughn School Supply

P.S. You might also like to visit the Special Features section of our website at **www.svschoolsupply.com** for other fun activities and learning suggestions.

Contents

Correlation to
Language Arts Content Standards . . 4

Story 1 . . . . **5**
A Facts and Inferences 8
B Summarizing 9
C Vocabulary 10
D Identifying and Interpreting
  Figurative Language 11

Story 2 . . . . **12**
A Facts and Inferences 16
B Skimming for Details 17
C Main Idea and Details 18
D Research Methods 20
E Sequencing 21
F Using a Time Chart:
  Skimming and Sequencing 22

Story 3 . . . . **23**
A Facts and Inferences 26
B Drawing Conclusions 27
C Vocabulary: Antonyms 28
D Vocabulary: Words in Context 28
E Reading for Different Purposes 29
F Facts and Opinions 30

Story 4 . . . . **32**
A Facts and Inferences 36
B Noting Details: Geographical Concepts 37
C Evaluating Materials to Determine Facts 38
D Identifying and Interpreting
  Figurative Language 40
E Vocabulary: Identifying Cultural Roots
  Through Research 40

Story 5 . . . . **41**
A Facts and Inferences 43
B Sequencing 44
C Vocabulary: Synonyms 45
D Vocabulary: Words in Context 45
E Cause and Effect 46

Skills Review
(Stories 1–5) **48**
A Main Idea, Predicting Outcomes 48
B Summarizing; Fact and Opinion 50
C Skimming for Main Idea; Research Methods . . 51
D Using a Time Chart,
  Skimming, and Sequencing 52
E Vocabulary: Antonyms 53
F Vocabulary: Synonyms 53
G Using a Table 54

Story 6 . . . . **55**
A Facts and Inferences 58
B Study Skill: Outlining 59
C Using a Circle Graph 60
D Identifying and Interpreting
  Figurative Language 61
E Making Comparisons/Analogies 62
F Vocabulary: Words in Context 63
G Vocabulary: Synonyms 63

Story 7 . . . . **64**
A Facts and Inferences 67
B Outline: Using Relevant Information 68
C Vocabulary: Words in Context 70
D Vocabulary: Crossword Puzzle 71
E Using a Time Line,
  Skimming, and Sequencing 72

Story 8 . . . . **73**
A Facts and Inferences 76
B Summarizing 77
C Main Idea and Details 78
D Vocabulary: Words in Context 80
E Drawing Conclusions, Predicting Outcomes . . 81
F Graphic Source: Comparing and Contrasting . 82

Story 9 . . . . **83**
A Facts and Inferences 86
B Inferences; Extending Vocabulary;
  Internet Literacy 87
C Vocabulary: Multiple Meanings 88

Skills Review
(Stories 6–9) **89**
A Main Idea 89
B Facts and Inferences 91
C Study Skill: Outlining 92
D Vocabulary: Words in Context 94
E Using a Circle Graph 95
F Vocabulary: Multiple Meanings 96

Story 10 . . . .**97**
A Facts and Inferences 100
B Drawing Conclusions: Meaning
   of Fairy Stories 101
C Identifying Story Elements;
   Plot and Character 102
D Vocabulary: Positive and Negative
   Meanings 103

Story 11 . . . .**104**
A Facts and Inferences 107
B Study Skills: Identifying Resources 108
C Study Skills: Using the Encyclopedia 109
D Study Skills: Using the Internet 110
E Identifying Fact or Fiction 111
F Study Skills: Identifying Relevance
   of Sources 113
G Vocabulary: Words in Context 114

Skills Review
(Stories 10–11) **115**
A Identifying Persuasive Arguments 115
B Evaluating Facts and
   Persuasive Arguments 116
C Identifying Story Elements:
   Character, Setting, and Mood 117
D Study Skills: Identifying Resources 118
E Drawing Conclusions 119

Answer Key **120**

Correlation to Language Arts Content Standards

LANGUAGE ARTS SKILLS	PAGE
Comprehension	
Author's Purpose, Audience	61, 86, 100, 101, 103, 107, 113, 116, 118,
Cause and Effect	44, 47, 81, 102
Compare and Contrast	59, 60, 61, 62, 82, 90
Drawing Conclusions	20, 21, 27, 37, 44, 49, 54, 60, 62, 81,103, 110, 113.116, 119.
Fact or Fiction	30, 38, 111, 114, 119
Facts and Inferences	8, 16, 26, 27, 29, 36, 43, 54, 58, 76, 86, 91, 100, 107, 119
Figurative Language	11, 40, 61, 101, 119
Identifying Fact and Opinion	30, 50, 111, 116, 119
Graphic Sources	22, 27, 29, 37, 52, 54, 60, 71, 72, 89, 90, 95
Main Ideas and Supporting Details	9, 17, 18, 21, 48, 51, 78, 89
Predicting Outcomes	7, 15, 21, 25, 35, 42, 49, 57, 66, 75, 99, 106
Relevant and Irrelevant Information	27, 44, 68, 80, 110, 114, 116, 117, 118
Sequencing	20, 22, 44, 47, 52, 72
Story Elements	8, 17, 21, 89, 102, 117
Vocabulary	
Analogies	11, 40, 61, 62
Antonyms	28, 53
Multiple Meanings	11, 40, 61, 62, 63, 71, 88, 96
Synonyms	45, 53, 63
Word Meaning	10, 40, 62, 70, 71, 72, 88, 96, 103, 117
Words in Context	10, 28, 63, 70, 80, 91, 94,114, 117
Research and Study Skills	
Encyclopedia	20, 109, 112
Evaluating Persuasive Methods	80, 103, 115, 116
Evaluating Resources	20, 40, 108, 110, 113, 118
Evaluating Text Organization	21, 44, 59, 68
Internet and Media Literacy	20, 87, 110, 111
Outlining	21, 59, 68, 69, 93
Skimming	17, 22, 31, 45, 54, 59, 68, 73, 96, 118
Summarizing	8, 9, 21, 52, 79

The Family Reunion

We have family reunions every July 4th. I can't remember any of them but one. It was last year when we met at the Llano River. That's when I learned to swim.

We arrived at my aunt's house on Friday night. My cousin J.W. was already there. J.W. is in high school. He is loud and funny, and a real pain. Every summer, he finds one of us younger kids and picks on us the whole time we are together. That year, it was my turn.

It started as soon as he saw me. "Hey, kid," he asked, "did you ever learn to swim? Are you going to do that doggy paddle thing again this year?" I hung my head down, embarrassed in front of my other cousins. My embarrassment didn't seem to bother J.W. He kept right on poking fun.

"You know, kid, you remind me a lot of Aunt Betty's cocker spaniel when you're in the water. Pant, splash, pant, splash. Don't get me wrong. I love it. It's a scream, and probably makes you popular with all of your friends back home. That's how everyone swims there, right?" I slipped away as quietly as I could, muttering, "J.W. is a conceited blowfish!"

The next morning, all the kids went down to the river right after breakfast. I sat around with the grown-ups. I couldn't bring myself to go down to the river. I kept talking to myself, building up my courage. It took until lunchtime for me to find it.

I grabbed a towel from the bathroom closet, put on my flip-flops, and marched down to the river. I may look like a cocker spaniel, but who cared? It was just J.W. talking, and his opinion, I didn't need. Most of my cousins were in the water, splashing, tubing, and diving for pennies.

The afternoon sun was warm and made the water feel great. I dragged one of the inner tubes on the bank into the water and plopped inside it. I wasn't afraid to float down the rapids in a tube. It was fun, and I stayed on the surface of the water, even when the rapids were fast.

As I floated near the rapids, I saw my cousin Danny. He's a little guy and always funny to watch. He was too small for the tube and sat low. When the water shot him across the rocks, Danny bumped all the way down the river. He always got out at the end of the rapids rubbing his backside. He didn't seem to mind, though. Danny was always the first one to run back up the riverbank to get ahead of the rapids and start again.

Just below the rapids, the river had carved a deep swimming hole. I pulled my tube out of the water and watched my cousins playing from the bank. I really wanted to be out there with them, but what was the point? There was J.W., splashing, laughing, and dunking the little kids under the water. No way was I going out there. I was in agony.

About the time I was getting ready to leave, Donnie, my brother, swam over to the bank. He sat with me in a shallow place near some large rocks. We basked in the hot sun. The water was really warm there. We talked about the river, about swimming, and about J.W. Then Donnie did something surprising. He leaned over and whispered in my ear, "If you want to learn to swim, I'll help you." The idea sounded great to me. "Can you teach me now?" I was enthusiastic. I remember that made Donnie laugh. "Hold on there, little spaniel, let's get in deeper water first," he said as he smiled.

We walked over to an area that was not too deep. Donnie showed me how to hold my face in the water and turn it to the side to breathe. I wasn't crazy about putting my face in the water at first. I had to practice for a while, but Donnie didn't seem to mind.

Next, he showed me how to move my arms in a big circle. Then we put breathing and circling together. When I could do both things at the same time, I thought I was ready. I didn't know what was coming next.

We moved into deeper water. I could still feel the river bottom squishing between my toes. Donnie told me to float on my back. That was easy. Then he told me to turn over and float on my stomach. That was hard. All of a sudden, water rushed into my nose. I couldn't breathe and I panicked. I started imitating a cocker spaniel again, a frightened one. So Donnie pulled my head up and helped me stand. I couldn't stop coughing and spitting out water. I think I spit out a tadpole, but Donnie told me I was imagining things. "Don't worry," Donnie said, "that was just your initiation dunk."

When I looked up along the bank, I saw my mom and dad watching me. At first, my mom looked worried, but then I saw her smile. Her smile made me determined. I told Donnie I was ready to try again. We stayed in the water so long that my fingers shriveled like old raisins. At first, I swam circles around Donnie. Then the circles got bigger and bigger. I knew how to swim!

When I was too tired to move anymore, I swam back to where Donnie sat on the bank. By the time I got there, all of my cousins were there, too. Even J.W. was there. He helped me out of the water, slapped me on the back, and said, "Hey, little spaniel, you're not a puppy anymore." That was J.W.'s idea of a compliment, and I was glad to take it.

What happened next?

How do you think J.W. and the writer's relationship changed? Write a short paragraph predicting what you think happened during the rest of the holiday.

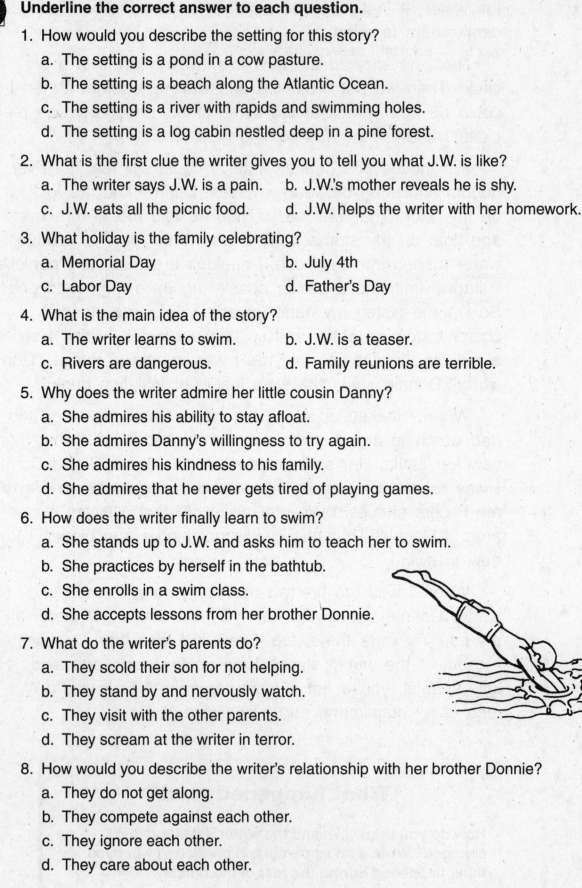

A   **Underline the correct answer to each question.**

1. How would you describe the setting for this story?
   a. The setting is a pond in a cow pasture.
   b. The setting is a beach along the Atlantic Ocean.
   c. The setting is a river with rapids and swimming holes.
   d. The setting is a log cabin nestled deep in a pine forest.

2. What is the first clue the writer gives you to tell you what J.W. is like?
   a. The writer says J.W. is a pain.   b. J.W.'s mother reveals he is shy.
   c. J.W. eats all the picnic food.   d. J.W. helps the writer with her homework.

3. What holiday is the family celebrating?
   a. Memorial Day   b. July 4th
   c. Labor Day   d. Father's Day

4. What is the main idea of the story?
   a. The writer learns to swim.   b. J.W. is a teaser.
   c. Rivers are dangerous.   d. Family reunions are terrible.

5. Why does the writer admire her little cousin Danny?
   a. She admires his ability to stay afloat.
   b. She admires Danny's willingness to try again.
   c. She admires his kindness to his family.
   d. She admires that he never gets tired of playing games.

6. How does the writer finally learn to swim?
   a. She stands up to J.W. and asks him to teach her to swim.
   b. She practices by herself in the bathtub.
   c. She enrolls in a swim class.
   d. She accepts lessons from her brother Donnie.

7. What do the writer's parents do?
   a. They scold their son for not helping.
   b. They stand by and nervously watch.
   c. They visit with the other parents.
   d. They scream at the writer in terror.

8. How would you describe the writer's relationship with her brother Donnie?
   a. They do not get along.
   b. They compete against each other.
   c. They ignore each other.
   d. They care about each other.

B Now, practice summarizing the story. Summarizing, or paraphrasing, helps you understand and remember what you read. It also helps you notice the main idea and important details of the story.

What happened first in the story?

What happened next in the story?

What happened last in the story?

What important lesson did you learn in the story?

C Write the correct word from the Word Box next to each meaning. If you have trouble choosing an answer, look back to the story to see how the word is used.

Word Box

reunions	dunking	imitating
initiation	shallow	enthusiastic
conceited	basked	compliment
rapids	panicked	shriveled
agony	squishing	embarrassment

---

1. not very deep _____

2. to think highly of oneself _____

3. felt fear, anxiety _____

4. meetings _____

5. a positive statement _____

6. dried up _____

7. acting, pretending to be like _____

8. an introduction to something new _____

9. fast-moving water _____

10. pushing under _____

11. excited _____

12. warmed oneself _____

13. uneasy feeling _____

14. squirting _____

15. great pain _____

Use each word in a sentence of your own.

conceited _____

enthusiastic _____

initiation _____

D Below are some words and phrases that could be described as "colorful language." Can you figure out the meaning of the underlined phrases? Look for clues to their meaning by reading the whole sentence or short paragraph carefully. Write what you think the meaning is on the lines.

1. J.W. is in high school. He is loud and funny, and <u>a real pain</u>. Every summer, he finds one of us younger kids and picks on us the whole time we are together.

   _____

   _____

2. Because of television and Internet broadcasts that go all over the globe, the <u>world is a smaller place</u>.

   _____

   _____

3. Principal Jones gave a speech to the whole class about helping to keep the school clean. He talked about our taking pride in the environment. Finally, he asked us to <u>give a hand</u> to his latest school clean-up project.

   _____

   _____

4. Sarah is an amazing person and a really good friend. She would <u>walk a mile for me</u> if I asked her to.

   _____

   _____

5. Karim didn't seem to get along very well at school at first. His grandmother said he was <u>a square peg in a round hole</u>. That made Karim mad, so he joined the band and made some good friends.

   _____

   _____

6. The hikers had walked all day and then set up their camp. When they finally settled down in their sleeping bags that night, they <u>slept like rocks.</u>

   _____

   _____

A Surprise for Cole

Cole's dad was unusually late picking him up on Friday night. Cole didn't say anything to his mother, but he was a little worried. His dad was never late. Cole sat quietly, tracing the stitching in his overnight bag. Finally, the phone rang. Cole's mom rushed to the kitchen to answer it. "He's on his way," she announced with relief. "He got tied up at the office."

Soon Cole and his dad were in the car driving to his dad's apartment. "Sorry about that, Cole," his dad said. "Something came up at the office. I know it's too late to do much tonight. But," he added, "I have a special day planned tomorrow. I hope you don't mind."

"It's okay, Dad," Cole said quickly. Cole knew that their weekends together were as important to his dad as they were to him.

The next morning, golden rays spilled through Cole's bedroom window. Saturday had come. By the time his dad got up, Cole was already dressed and eating breakfast. "Wow," his dad said. "You're in a hurry this morning." His dad smiled. "Let me finish this cup of coffee, and we'll be on our way, okay?" Cole nodded.

The highway was a gray stripe through green countryside. On either side, wildflowers bounced in the wind. Their red and yellow heads moved up and down like fishing bobs on a lake. Cole's dad slowed the car and turned right onto a farm road. Then he turned again, this time onto a dirt road that sliced the pasture.

Cole's dad stopped the car. "Well, what do you think?" Cole looked puzzled. "What do you mean?" he asked.

His dad laughed softly. "This is our farm. This is why I was late last night. I had to sign the papers." Cole looked amazed. His eyes widened and his mouth fell open, but he couldn't speak a word.

Cole and his dad walked through the pasture to a row of graceful trees. The deep green live oaks and giant cottonwoods bowed over a narrow creek. The creek babbled like a child. The sun's rays sparkled on the water. Cole and his dad sat on the bank. "What do you think, Cole?" Cole turned slowly, forcing his eyes away from the creek. "I love it," he almost whispered.

Cole's dad took him towards the old farmhouse beyond the creek. "I thought we could come here on the weekends, Cole. We could fix up the house together. I could use the help. Wait until you see it. It's been empty for more than forty years."

 "Who lived here then, Dad?" Cole asked. "I don't know," said his dad. "The agent said the last owner never used the house. He just let it fall down. He's the person who sold the farm." They reached the farmhouse, and for the second time in one day, Cole didn't know what to say. This was the tallest, oldest, most run-down house he'd ever seen. He loved it.

"Wow!" Cole yelled. "Cool house! This is great!" Cole started running. His dad yelled, "Cole, slow down. You can't trust those steps. Wait." But Cole couldn't hear the last warning. It came just as Cole's leg went through a rotten step. The bottom half of his body disappeared, swallowed by the steps. Cole's Dad raced toward him. "Are you okay, Cole? Can you move?" he asked, with panic in his voice.

Cole groaned a little as his dad pulled him from the step. "I'm fine, really. I don't think anything's broken." While his dad checked his legs, Cole lay on the porch. His head turned toward the jagged hole. "Dad, I think there's something in there. Look." Cole's dad ignored him as he continued to ask what hurt.

"Dad, what is it?" Cole said. He'd forgotten about his legs. Cole's dad looked inside the hole. "I don't know, Cole, but you stay here. I'll go in this time." He squeezed through the hole, landing with a thud. When he came back up, he had a box caked in decades of dirt. He and Cole used a pocketknife to remove the dirt and pick the small, rusting lock that kept the box sealed.

"Wow," Cole and his dad said at the same time. Inside were a small leather box and a dirty envelope. Inside the box was a World War II Medal of Honor. Even now, the eagle shined, and the ribbon looked fresh. Inside the envelope was a certificate and a single photograph. "Horace Mickel," Cole's dad said as he read the name on the certificate. "I'd say this medal and this house must have belonged to him."

"Who was Horace Mickel, Dad? Do you think he left anything else under those steps?" Cole asked. "Or in the house?" he added eagerly.

"I don't know," Cole's dad chuckled. "Let's forget the steps for now. If you think you can get yourself up, we'll start looking for the answers to your questions inside." Cole's dad unlocked the front door. He held Cole's elbow as Cole hobbled inside. The wind came with them, disturbing dust that had sat comfortably for forty years. Spider webs as fine as lace capped their heads. "This is great, Dad. It looks like Mr. Mickel left everything behind. There are bound to be clues everywhere."

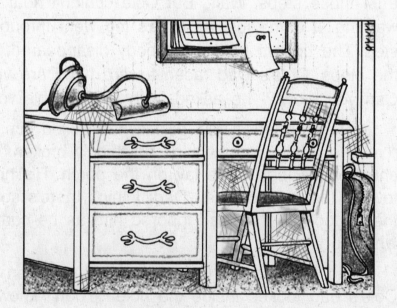

"I think you're right, Cole. But I have an idea. Let's not try to find all of our answers today. Let's make this last awhile. Let's make this our weekend project, and we'll come to know Mr. Mickel a little at a time, just like friends normally do." Cole's dad hugged him hard.

"Good idea, Dad. I think I'll put this photograph above the fireplace. Then we'll know where to find Mr. Mickel when we come back."

What will it look like?

Use clues that you picked up while reading the story to write a short paragraph. Describe what the farmhouse will look like when Cole and his dad finish fixing it up.

Underline the correct answer to each question.

1. How do you know Cole and his mom are nervous?

   a. Cole and his mother argue with each other.

   b. Cole paces back and forth while his mom watches television.

   c. Cole bites his fingernails while his mom looks angry.

   d. Cole sits sadly while his mother rushes to get the phone.

2. Why was Cole's dad late to pick him up?

   a. He forgot to get gas.

   b. He was held up by a storm.

   c. He had a meeting.

   d. He had to sign papers.

3. What is Cole's surprise?

   a. the country drive   b. the farm

   c. the beautiful wildflowers   d. the early breakfast

4. What did Cole do when he ran onto the farmhouse steps?

   a. He met the farmer's wife.

   b. He rang the doorbell.

   c. He fell through the steps.

   d. He picked up the newspaper.

5. What did Cole and his dad find hidden under the steps?

   a. an arrowhead   b. a locked box

   c. an old bicycle   d. a jar of pennies

6. When do Cole and his dad plan to work on the farmhouse?

   a. in the early morning, during the week

   b. in the summer vacation

   c. in the evening, during the week

   d. on weekends

7. Where will Cole's dad probably live until the farmhouse is fixed up?

   a. in his apartment   b. in a hotel

   c. in a duplex   d. in a house

8. Where did Cole place the photograph?

   a. on the wall

   b. on the end table

   c. on the fireplace mantel

   d. in his wallet

Details in a story tell **where, when, why, how, who,** and **what** about the topic and/or the action. Skim the story to find these details or facts. Write the key words that help you locate the information, and then answer the questions. One is done for you.

1. What color were the wildflowers along the highway?

   highway—red and yellow

2. Name the kinds of trees on the farm.

3. How many years had the farmhouse been empty?

4. Who told Cole's dad about the former owner?

5. What did Cole and his dad use to open the box?

6. What is Cole's overnight bag a clue to?

In 1863, President Lincoln first awarded the Congressional Medal of Honor. It was created to encourage the Union soldiers in the Civil War and "increase efficiency in the navy." Many decades have passed, and the medal has grown into a special symbol of bravery and sacrifice. Today, the Medal of Honor is the highest U.S. military decoration given.

In 1918, Congress defined what is expected of a Medal of Honor winner. Congress said that the person had to be a member of the military. Congress also said the person must be engaged in conflict with an enemy of the United States. And, finally, and most important, the person should show bravery and risk to his or her life "above and beyond the call of duty."

Of the millions of Americans who have gone into battle, only a little over 3,000 have been given the Medal of Honor. Most of the people who have received the Medal of Honor did not survive the battle for which they were honored. A few did, however. All of these medal holders, living or dead, have shown their bravery by going into heavy fire or going behind enemy lines. Some have even given their lives to save their fellow soldiers.

By 1963, the requirements for the Navy, the Army, and the Air Force were made the same. Today, only the designs of the medals differ from one branch of the service to the other. All three feature an inverted, gold star. They hang from blue ribbons that can be worn around the neck. Each ribbon ends in a "knot" that is embroidered with thirteen stars. These stars represent the thirteen original American colonies. The Air Force and Army medals hang from a bar that reads "valor." The Navy medal hangs from an anchor.

The Medal of Honor has changed from being a simple reward. The medal has grown into something much more valued and respected. It is only for those who have risked their lives in an outstanding way for the sake of others. During World War II, more Medals of Honor were given to the dead than to the living. This was true during the Korean War and the Vietnam War, too. This has given the medal a special serious quality. The living Medal of Honor holders know that they are lucky. They rarely speak of glory; they mainly speak of their gratitude. They do not say they "won" the medal. They prefer to say that they and their fellow soldiers "earned" it.

Each paragraph about the Medal of Honor has two or more details that support a main idea. Read the following ideas from the five paragraphs in the story. Label each Main Idea or Detail.

Paragraph 1.

_____ a. The medal was created to encourage the Union soldiers.

_____ b. The medal is the highest military decoration awarded.

_____ c. President Lincoln first awarded the Medal of Honor.

Paragraph 2.

_____ a. The person must be a member of the military.

_____ b. The person must be engaged in conflict with the enemy.

_____ c. The person must show bravery "above and beyond."

_____ d. Congress defined what is expected.

Paragraph 3.

_____ a. All medal holders have shown their bravery.

_____ b. Only a little over 3,000 Medals of Honor have been given.

_____ c. Most soldiers did not survive the battle.

_____ d. A few soldiers did survive.

Paragraph 4.

_____ a. All three medals have an inverted, gold star.

_____ b. Only the designs differ from one branch to another.

_____ c. The Navy medal hangs from an anchor.

Paragraph 5.

_____ a. Medal holders prefer to say they "earned" it.

_____ b. The medal has a special serious quality.

_____ c. They rarely speak of glory.

_____ d. They speak of gratitude.

D Who is Horace Mickel and what happened to him? Cody found a box with a Medal of Honor belonging to Horace hidden under the step. Think about the clues given in the story that Cody could pursue.

1. If Cody wants to find out more about Horace Mickel, what research tools would you suggest he use?

_____

_____

_____

_____

2. What do you think he should do first in his search for the identity of Mr. Mickel?

_____

_____

_____

3. What should he do second?

_____

_____

_____

_____

4. What should he do third?

_____

_____

_____

_____

E Do you think Cody will find out who Horace Mickel is? Who do you think he will turn out to be? Is Horace still alive? How old would he be?

Consider writing a story about Cody's search for Horace Mickel. Think about a main idea for your story. Use the boxes below to help you organize your ideas and the order of what will happen in your story.

What is the main idea of your story?

What happens first?

What happens next?

How does your story end?

Most autobiographies and biographies are arranged in a logical order, by date. Dates are important in doing research. They can help you skim a passage and create an outline of information quickly. You can scan for important happenings by noticing the dates in a passage. Read this short biography of a Medal of Honor holder and fill out the Time Chart below.

The Medal of Honor of all three branches of the service have a woman's face on them. The Army and Navy have the Greek goddess Athena. The Air Force features the face of the Statue of Liberty. Despite this, Dr. Mary Walker is the only woman ever awarded a Medal of Honor.

Mary Walker became a doctor in 1855. After the Battle of Bull Run in 1861, she helped take care of the 1,100 wounded. In 1863, Dr. Walker served close to the battlefield. She often went deep into enemy territory to deliver needed medical supplies.

She also performed an even more dangerous service. It is believed that she acted as a spy for Union troops against the Confederacy. She often rode behind enemy lines to discover and carry important information about enemy troop movements. In 1864, Dr. Walker was captured by the Confederate Army and held as a prisoner. She was released later that year in a prisoner exchange.

The Medal of Honor was given in 1865 to those who had shown "soldier-like qualities" in the Civil War. Dr. Mary Edwards Walker had certainly shown these qualities. President Andrew Johnson awarded her the medal.

In 1866, Dr. Walker began to speak out for women's right to vote. This was called the suffragette movement. She died in 1919, just months before the 19th Amendment was passed. This amendment gave women the right to vote.

Time Chart

Date	Event
1853	Mary Walker enrolls in medical school.
1855	

The Unwritten Laws

Sometimes it's hard being an older sister, especially when you have a brother like mine. He's so cheerful all the time. Plus, he's excited about starting middle school next year. It's only February, and he's still in fifth grade, but he's already excited. I've tried to tell him there's not so much to be excited about, but so far I haven't convinced him. The first lesson I tried to teach him was about lockers. You see, of all the reasons there are to go to middle school, my brother thinks having a locker is the best reason of all.

I have tried to explain that there are some middle-school laws that aren't written in any school handbook. They're not posted in the hallway or on the bulletin board in the office. They just exist. Only middle-school students know what they are. They're a secret to everyone else. So, I tried to explain the laws about lockers.

First, I told him he'd better start practicing deep-knee bends. I described the lockers at our school. Two rows of lockers line every hallway. One of the laws every middle-school kid knows is that the tall kids get the lockers on the bottom. If you're tall, and my brother is, then you ought to practice deep-knee bends every morning before you get to school. That will be the only thing that keeps you in shape. Plus, you'll have to learn how to bend with one arm up in the air. I explained that you use the arm to protect your head. That's because the rule that makes tall kids get the bottom lockers is the same rule that gives short kids the top lockers. While you're on your knees, I told him, they're on their toes. At least once a day, the kid on top loses his or her

balance. The kid's books fall with the kid, and there,
I say with a short demonstration, is where your arm comes
in handy.

He watched carefully and seemed to understand. I thought
I had convinced him that his first locker wasn't going to be
the highlight of middle school, but I was wrong. He smiled
and started doing deep-knee bends. He is really industrious!
He is amazing.

So I tried to give him another lesson in locker reality.
We talked about the locks. I explained that a lock never
works when you're in a hurry. It will work any other time,
but not if you're in a rush. That means if you don't remember
to get your track shoes out before you slam the door shut,
you're going to be late for gym. The coach isn't going to
listen to any excuses, and you and all the other kids who
couldn't get their lockers open will run extra laps. You can
blame the second law of lockers. Every middle-school kid
knows that a lock only has one good spin a day. After that,
you have to beg, scream, and fight to get it open. You also
have to be ready to take the consequences when you're late
for class.

I stopped to look at my brother again. His face looked
serious, so I thought I was getting through. Then, he started
stretching like you do before you run laps. Its hard to predict
what he will do. He persists when he needs to. He really
is amazing.

Okay, fine, laws one and two didn't seem to make much
difference, so I moved to the third law. That's the law of egg-
salad sandwiches. This law, I explained, says that if even one
kid in the whole school eats egg-salad for lunch, that kid has
the locker above yours. Your nose finds your locker before
you do. The smell attaches itself to everything in your locker,
including your gym clothes. People won't make fun of you, of
course. They know you didn't get to pick your locker.
However, you can't expect them to eat lunch with you.

I looked closely at my brother. His eyebrows met in the
middle. He seemed to be thinking hard. Then he ran into the

bathroom. When he came out, he had a can of air freshener in his hands. "This should take care of law number three," he said. I shook my head. I don't think I'm going to win this battle.

I had only one locker law left—the surprise clean-out. I explained that at least once in every grading period, your homeroom teacher makes the whole class clean out their lockers. You never know when these days are coming, and if you aren't prepared, the word *embarrassed* is not enough to describe how you feel. Middle-school teachers know just the right time for a clean-out. It's always the day that you forget to take home your dirty gym shorts. It's the day when your overdue library books are bursting to get out. It's the day a colony of fruit flies escapes from the science lab and finds the rotting apple in your locker. It's the day when the Valentine card you got for the girl who sits next to you in homeroom falls out and lands at the girl's feet.

I thought for sure that mentioning the Valentine card would do the trick. My brother gets bashful around girls. I waited for him to say something. He disappeared again, this time into his bedroom. When he came out, he handed me a card. I opened the card and read it aloud. It said, "To My Sister on Valentine's Day." My brother smiled and gave me a hug. Now I was embarrassed. What an amazing kid! He's going to love middle school.

What will happen next?

What do you think the brother's first day at middle-school will be like? Think about your own experience. Consider the brother's personality. Write a short paragraph describing his first day at school.

Underline the correct answer for each question.

1. What grade is the younger brother in?
   a. seventh grade
   b. fifth grade
   c. fourth grade
   d. sixth grade

2. What is the first unwritten law?
   a. Short people get the lockers on the top.
   b. Tall people get the lockers on the bottom.
   c. Don't leave egg-salad sandwiches in your locker.
   d. If something can go wrong, it will.

3. What is the second unwritten law?
   a. Practice deep-knee bends.
   b. Never lock your locker.
   c. A lock never opens when you are in a hurry.
   d. Always keep your locker clean.

4. How does the brother act around girls?
   a. bashful
   b. talkative
   c. comfortable
   d. quiet

5. Why does the sister keep calling her brother "amazing"?
   a. He is a magician and does magic tricks.
   b. He is a big pest.
   c. He exercises and is in good shape.
   d. He is so cheerful and excited about middle school.

6. What did the younger brother give his sister at the end of the story?
   a. a Valentine's card
   b. flowers
   c. candy
   d. his baseball cards

B The brother and sister in "The Unwritten Laws" are siblings. This means they are children of the same parents, or have at least one parent in common. Use the diagram below of a family tree to answer the questions about the family of Tamisha and Will Locker.

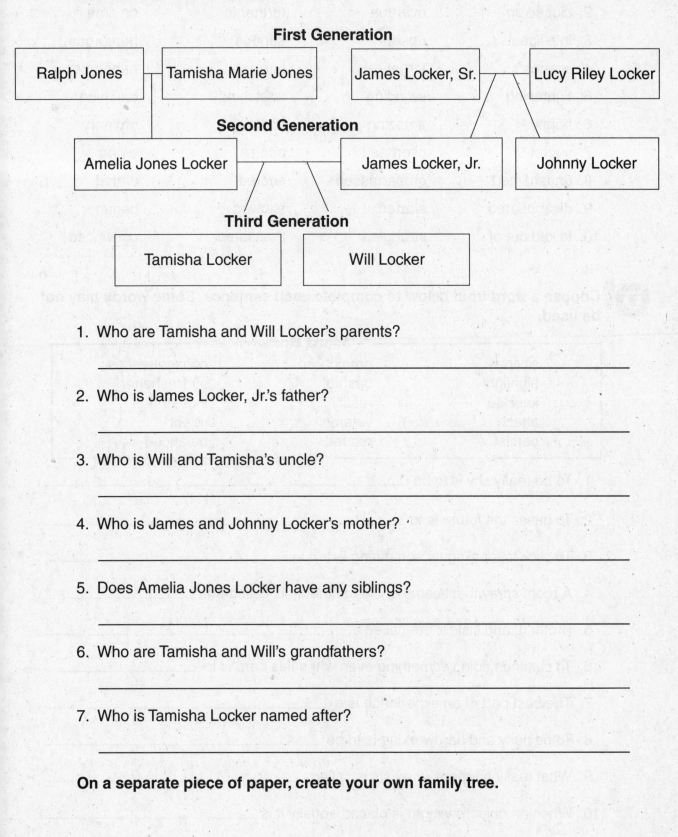

First Generation

Ralph Jones — Tamisha Marie Jones

James Locker, Sr. — Lucy Riley Locker

Second Generation

Amelia Jones Locker — James Locker, Jr.

Johnny Locker

Third Generation

Tamisha Locker

Will Locker

1. Who are Tamisha and Will Locker's parents?

_____

2. Who is James Locker, Jr.'s father?

_____

3. Who is Will and Tamisha's uncle?

_____

4. Who is James and Johnny Locker's mother?

_____

5. Does Amelia Jones Locker have any siblings?

_____

6. Who are Tamisha and Will's grandfathers?

_____

7. Who is Tamisha Locker named after?

_____

On a separate piece of paper, create your own family tree.

On each line are two words that are antonyms, or opposite in meaning. Circle the antonyms.

1. cheerful   abrupt   depressed   talkative
2. closed up   overdue   farther in   on time
3. intelligent   upset   serious   humorous
4. scatter   forget   late   remember
5. tightening   swinging   stretching   teaching
6. happy   amazing   spotless   ordinary
7. secret   overhead   open   swing
8. unashamed   embarrassed   snared   dirtied
9. disappeared   started   showed   began
10. talked out of   struggled   pressured   convinced

 Choose a word from below to complete each sentence. Some words may not be used.

Word Box

siblings	predict	consequences
highlight	bashful	air freshener
knuckle	reality	industrious
attach	veteran	reject
persist	related	balanced
---

1. To be really shy is to be _____.

2. To guess the future is to _____.

3. To stick to, or cling to, something is to _____.

4. A room spray that scents or cleans the air is called an _____.

5. Brothers and sisters are called _____.

6. To continue doing something even when it is hard is to _____.

7. The best part of an experience is a _____.

8. To be busy and hardworking is to be _____.

9. What really happens or exists is called _____.

10. When an object's weight is placed equally it is _____.

E The sister in "The Unwritten Laws" tries to pass along to her brother ideas on how to survive in middle school. Most schools have a handbook that lets students know the rules for their school. Read the passage from a school handbook and answer the questions.

Library Information

Mrs. Mitchell, the school librarian, would like all students to know that they are expected to adopt a quiet manner when using the library. Students are studying and reading and need a good atmosphere to work in.

General student hours are:
Monday–Wednesday 9 A.M.–4 P.M.
Thursday and Friday 8 A.M.–3:30 P.M.
Bus students only:
Monday–Friday 7 A.M.–8 A.M.

On Tuesday afternoons at 3:00, a "homework help" math study group meets in the library's Sierra Room. A student must have a pass from the principal and a note from parents or guardians. If you would like to join, you need to put your name on a sign-up sheet in Mrs. Mitchell's office.

Have a written list of math questions and problems ready to show Mrs. Mitchell.

---

1. How late is the library open on Tuesdays? _____

2. Who is the library open to from 7 A.M. to 8 A.M.? _____

3. What 3 pieces of paper must you have in order to participate in homework help?

   _____

   _____

   _____

4. What piece of paper should you sign? _____

5. What list do you need to prepare for Mrs. Mitchell?

   _____

6. When does the library open on Thursdays to all students? _____

7. Where does the homework help group meet? _____

8. Why are students expected to be quiet in the library?

   _____

   _____

F When you research a subject, you usually can find many facts about it. Sometimes you may find information that is someone else's opinion. Being able to tell the difference between what is fact and what is opinion is important. Remember, an **opinion** is **a belief or feeling about something**. Now, read a story about two famous brothers.

The Wright Brothers

When they were little boys, the Wright brothers' father brought home a strange toy. The boys probably thought it looked something like a bird and something like a bat. It was made of paper and wood and used a twisted rubber band for power. When it was tossed into the air, it would fly across the room. When the toy broke, the two boys, Wilbur and Orville, experimented and made their own flying toys. From then on, they were interested and excited by anything that could fly. It was 1878 and at that time there were no planes and no cars. People traveled by train, horse and buggy, and bicycle.

In 1893, the two young men started a bicycle shop. Only a few cars were beginning to be seen around town. The cars made so much racket they shouldn't have been on the road anyway. But the brothers were more interested in planes and flying than in the motor car. They had read about a man named Otto Lilienthal who had built a plane that did not have an engine. He called it a glider. Unfortunately, Lilienthal and his glider crashed.

Orville and Wilbur weren't discouraged. They started reading everything they could about flying. They probably even read comic books about flying. They wrote to the Smithsonian Institution to ask for help. A man at the museum sent them all the latest books and papers about flying.

The two brothers had read that balance and control were key to flying a glider. But, how could an airplane be kept in balance? How could a pilot control the plane, making it go up and down, or left and right? They should have known that it would take a long time to understand these things.

They decided that the wings of the plane should be flexible and movable at the ends. One wing could be curved up by a control, while the other was curved down. In this way, the wings would meet the air at different angles, and one would get greater lift from the air than the other. This would make it possible to steer and balance the plane. They also decided they needed something called a rudder. Like on a boat, the rudder would be a flat piece on the back of the plane. By moving it from side to side, the glider could be steered by a pilot.

The two went to work and built a model of their idea. They flew the small glider like a kite. From the ground below, they were able to work its controls by pulling on ropes attached to its wings and rudder. The experiment was a success, and their model flew. They must have been happy on that day.

By 1900, they had finished work on their life-size glider. They chose Kitty Hawk in North Carolina for the flight test. At first, their glider went only a few feet. As they experimented and adjusted the controls, the flights kept getting longer.

Then, in 1903, they built a plane with an engine. Again, they went to the soft sands of Kitty Hawk to test it. They wanted to be the first men to fly a powered airplane. Early on the morning of December 17, 1903, the two brothers were ready. They had worked so long and so closely on their dream, Orville and Wilbur tossed a coin to see who would try to fly the plane. Orville won the toss.

It was very windy, and Orville had a difficult time controlling the airplane. Orville ought to have known he would need great upper-body strength. But, even though the flying machine only went 100 feet and stayed in the air twelve seconds, it was enough. Orville had made the first powered flight in history. Wilbur went up next and managed to stay in the air almost a minute!

The two brothers, overjoyed with what they had done together, sent a telegram. It was to the person who had started their passion for flying so long ago. They wired their father, "Success. Four flights. Inform press. Home Christmas."

Put an F by each fact from the story and an O by each opinion from the story.

_____ 1. The boys probably thought the toy looked something like a bird and something like a bat.

_____ 2. People traveled by train, horse and buggy, and bicycle.

_____ 3. In 1893, the two young men opened a bicycle shop.

_____ 4. The cars made so much racket they shouldn't have been on the road anyway.

_____ 5. They had read about a man named Otto Lilienthal who had built a plane that did not have an engine.

_____ 6. They started reading everything they could about flying.

_____ 7. They probably even read comic books about flying.

_____ 8. The two brothers had read that balance and control were key to flying a glider.

_____ 9. They should have known that it would take a long time to understand these things.

_____ 10. In this way, the wings would meet the air at different angles, and one would get greater lift from the air than the other.

_____ 11. Like on a boat, the rudder would be a flat piece on the back of the plane.

_____ 12. They flew the small glider like a kite.

_____ 13. They must have been happy on that day.

_____ 14. They chose Kitty Hawk in North Carolina for the flight test.

_____ 15. Orville ought to have known he would need great upper-body strength.

Cajun Celebration

For Les and Wes Bateaux, finding something interesting to do on the weekends wasn't hard. After all, they were easy to please. There were three things they loved most. The first was their dog, Poe. The second was being outside. The third was food, any kind of food. When you live in Cajun land, Louisiana, USA, the last two are easy to find. It's jambalaya country, after all! And Poe, well, Poe is easy to find, too. Look for the Bateaux brothers, and you'll find Poe either ahead or behind, chasing the scent of food.

Two weekends ago, the brothers and Poe went to a swamp festival near their home. Poe sat with them in their pirogue, or canoe, as they paddled through water filled with alligators. Ashore, the brothers took turns tossing popcorn shrimp to Poe. Poe made the brothers proud. He had, after all, learned to catch popcorn shrimp before he was even six months old. Now he never missed. A series of quick jaw snaps could take a pound of popcorn shrimp out of the air in minutes.

Last weekend, the brothers took Poe to a fair. Wes and Poe ate sour, mouth-pinching pickle chips while they watched Les lose at the ring toss. Les had never been very good at ring tosses, so Wes tried. It didn't take long before Wes won a life-sized stuffed alligator. What better way to celebrate such a victory than with the beignets they loved so much? Each bite into these fried pillows of dough sent clouds of powdered sugar into the air.

This weekend the brothers were in the mood for another fair. It was already Friday, and they didn't have any plans. Wes was starting to think they might have to stay at home when he heard Les drive up to the house.

Poe came in first. Then came Les. Both of them looked like soaked muskrats. "Whew," Les said as he took off his rain hat and hung it on a hook by the door. Poe shook hard, sending arrows of water in every direction. "Look, Wes!" said Les, pointing to a flyer he held in his hand. "I found one! The Frog Festival is tomorrow. Do you remember how close we came to winning the frog-racing contest last year? Let's try again this year. What do you say?"

"I don't know," said Wes. "If it's raining like this tomorrow, we may have to hop like frogs just to get there. Heck. Let's go anyway. We'd better visit the creek to find a new frog."

"Yee-hah!" Les yelled, as he slapped his leg. "Come on, Poe. Let's go. There's nothing like a rain to bring out the frogs." Les grabbed his hat and a fishing bucket off the porch as he and Poe headed to the creek. "Come on, Wes, it's getting dark. If we're going to find a winner, we need to start now."

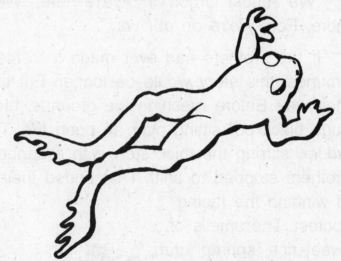

Saturday arrived, and the two brothers and Poe jumped into their truck. The sky didn't own a single cloud, and the air smelled of magnolia flowers and barbecue. The brothers were excited when they saw how many people had shown up for the fair.

At the ticket counter, Les bought the tickets while Wes asked where to sign up for the frog-racing contest. "If it's the frog-racing you want, you'd better hurry," said the lady selling tickets. "The contest is about to start. You'll need to sign in and get a number for your frog. The frog-jumping contest comes later. You have plenty of time before you have to sign up for that one."

"We want the first one," Les said. "We've got a winner, I know it."

On their way to the racing grounds, the brothers and Poe passed booth after booth of spicy treats. Red pepper and other spices tickled their noses. Blackened catfish sizzled on grills. Curls of pink shrimp floated in giant soup pots. The brothers' eyes widened to take it all in. There were shelves lined with orange sweet-potato pies. There were bowls as big as kitchen sinks filled with steaming black-eyed peas, tomatoes, and okra. Tables held stacks of fried crab cakes bigger than dessert plates. There was no end to the food. The brothers were frozen with delight until Poe barked sharply. The brothers jumped like nervous frogs at the noise.

"We almost forgot why we're here," Wes said. "Say no more, Poe. We're on our way."

If the brothers had ever made it to the frog-racing grounds, this story would be longer. But the jambalaya got in their way. Before reaching the grounds, the brothers passed a huge black pot sitting over an open fire. The cook stood on a ladder, stirring the thick stew with a canoe paddle. The brothers stopped to sniff. That ended their frog's chances of winning the racing contest. The smells of sweet rice, shrimp, crab, and oysters held the brothers captive. Even Poe seemed to have lost all interest in the race.

"You know, Wes, surely by now that race has started, don't you think? There's no point in going over there now."

"I think you're right, Les. Poe, let's stop here awhile and give our new green friend a chance to stretch his legs. He needs to warm up before the jumping contest this afternoon. Speaking of warming up, I'm ready for some jambalaya. What about you?"

"I'm ready," Wes said with excitement. "I don't think weekends ever get better than this, do you?" he asked. The brothers watched Poe wag his tail and lick his lips. "See," said Wes, "even Poe agrees."

What will happen next?

Think about what you have learned about the two brothers, Wes and Les. Write a paragraph to describe what you think the brothers and Poe did the weekend after the Frog Festival.

Underline the correct answer to each question.

1. How do you know that the brothers love food?
   a. They have published a recipe book.
   b. They are always chasing after food.
   c. They fish and hunt for food in the swamp.
   d. They are covered in crumbs and powdered sugar.

2. What are the names of the main characters?
   a. Moe, Bo, and Tess
   b. Les, Wes, and Poe
   c. Larry, Gary, and Cy
   d. John, James, and Rover

3. What dangerous animals swim through the swamp?
   a. alligators
   b. anacondas
   c. giant squids
   d. sharks

4. Les loses at what kind of fair game?
   a. clown dunk
   b. bobbing for apples
   c. ring toss
   d. archery

5. What flyer did Les pick up?
   a. The Pickle Chip Contest flyer
   b. The Alligator Snap Fair flyer
   c. The Crab Cake Bake flyer
   d. The Frog Festival flyer

6. What did the trio need to do before they could participate in the contest?
   a. get permission from the contest organizer
   b. sign in and get a number
   c. join in a test race
   d. sing a cajun song

7. Why didn't the brothers make it to the racing contest?
   a. They decided to listen to the music instead.
   b. They had car trouble.
   c. Their canoe overturned.
   d. They were sidetracked by the spicy food.

B Where in the world are Wes and Les Bateaux? Try to answer the questions without looking back at the story. Look at the map. Then answer the following questions.

1. On what continent does the story happen? _____

2. In what country does the story happen? _____

3. In what state does the story happen? _____

4. How would you describe the geography of Wes and Les Bateaux's area?

   _____

5. What other words are used in the story to name the area Wes and Les are in?

   _____

   _____

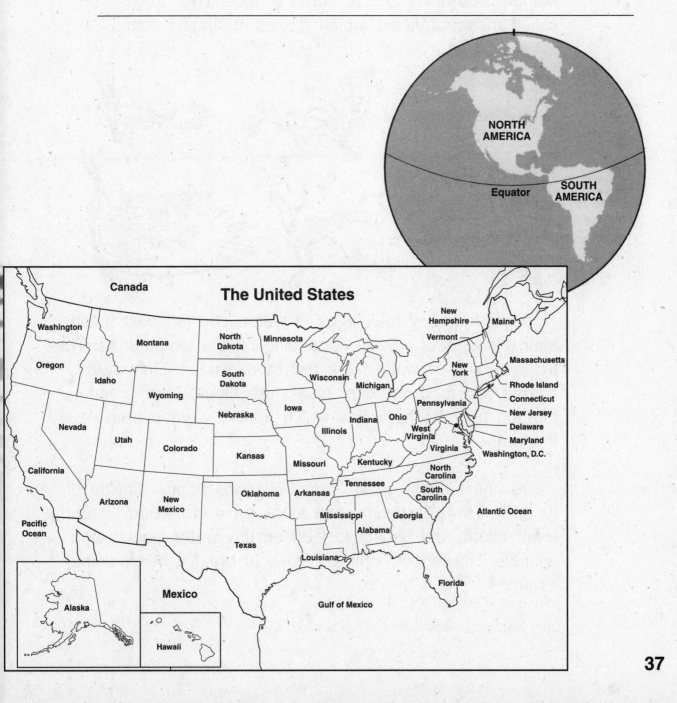

Fascinating Frogs

The typical frog is a neckless, wide-mouthed, long-legged leaper. It has tiny teeth, and it cannot chew well. Its mouth must be large enough to swallow prey whole. Its hind legs are very long and strong for take-off when leaping. Its small padded front legs, or arms, take up the shock of landing.

A frog goes through many changes in its journey to adulthood. First it changes from a round jelly-like egg to a tadpole with a tail and no arms or legs. This process is called *metamorphosis*, which means "changing shape."

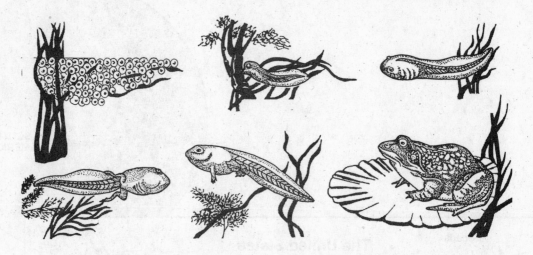

Most frogs lay their eggs in water. The tadpoles hatch after a couple of weeks, depending on the temperature. The tadpoles stay in water for a few more weeks. They swim around and feed on water plants like algae. They breathe through their feathery gills which absorb oxygen from the water.

As the tadpole grows, many changes happen inside of its body. The gills shrink, and lungs grow in its body. It eats fewer plants and begins to feed on tiny water insects and animals. The tadpole starts to take in breaths of air using its lungs.

As the tadpole begins to get its limbs, its tail begins to shrink and is absorbed into the body. Its legs usually start to develop first, and then the arms. Finally, the tadpole is a tiny froglet, breathing air and hunting its prey in and out of the water.

Even though all frogs have arms and legs, not all can leap. Some frogs walk, some crawl, and some run or hop. Certain tree frogs can even fly, or glide, from tree to tree. Almost all frogs have sticky pads on their hands and feet. They use these to cling to plants and trees.

Some frogs, like the Mascarenes, leap in a long series of rapid jumps. A related species holds the world's record in distance jumping for frogs. It jumped 33.5 feet (10.2 m) in three jumps!

Write true on the line if the detail is true. Write false if the detail is not true.

_____ 1. A frog begins life as round, jelly-like egg.

_____ 2. A typical frog chews its prey at least thirty-two times.

_____ 3. The process of a frog changing from egg to adult is called metamorphosis.

_____ 4. Just after tadpoles hatch, they feed on tiny insects.

_____ 5. Tadpoles absorb oxygen through their long, feathery tail.

_____ 6. Adult frogs breathe through the soft pads on their hands and feet.

_____ 7. The tadpole changes into a froglet.

_____ 8. Some frogs can fly, or glide, from tree to tree.

_____ 9. Frogs have mouths that are wide enough to swallow prey whole.

_____ 10. The arms of a frog are designed to take the shock of landing.

_____ 11. Most frogs have sticky pads on their hands and feet.

_____ 12. A record-holding frog jumped an incredible 33.5 feet in one jump.

D A simile is a comparison of two things using *like* or *as*. A metaphor is a comparison of two things that are not very similar. The words *like* and *as* are not used. Read the sentences below. Write an **M** next to each metaphor and an **S** next to each simile.

_____ 1. He bit into fried pillows of dough.

_____ 2. Clouds of powdered sugar floated around.

_____ 3. They looked like two soaked muskrats.

_____ 4. The rainbow was a promise of better times.

_____ 5. The pink shrimp danced on the boiling water like ballerinas.

_____ 6. The two boys made pigs of themselves.

_____ 7. They were as late as yesterday.

_____ 8. The grill sizzled and sounded like rain.

_____ 9. The swamp was a monster of mud.

_____10. Alligators swam just below the surface like bumpy submarines.

E The writer in "Cajun Celebration" uses some unusual words like *pirogue* and *jambalaya*. These words, although a part of English usage, have their beginnings in other cultures. Use your dictionary or Internet skills to look up the words below. Write on the line next to each word the country or culture where the word began and the word's definition. One has been done for you.

1. Cajun __**Acadian French—a native of Louisiana**_____

2. pirogue _____

3. beignet _____

4. jambalaya _____

5. barbecue _____

6. metamorphosis _____

7. festival _____

8. metaphor _____

9. Louisiana _____

A Law of Motion

Sir Isaac Newton was an English mathematician and scientist who lived in the 1600s and 1700s. He published his three laws of motion, which describe how forces affect the motion of an object, in 1687. You can demonstrate one of Newton's laws of motion with an apparatus called a Newton's cradle. The cradle will show that things at rest tend to stay at rest until acted on by an outside force. A Newton's cradle also demonstrates what scientists call the "Principle of Conservation of Energy." That means that energy is never created or destroyed. Energy can change from one form to another, but the total amount of energy stays the same.

It is easier to understand these scientific principles if you use your own Newton's cradle. You need only a few materials to build one. They are:

- 1 ruler marked in inches
- 1 pencil or dowel rod
- scissors
- 5 paper clips
- 5 8-in. pieces of fishing line
- 5 wooden beads

Once you have your materials, you are ready to begin building. Here's how.

First, use your ruler to make five marks on the pencil or dowel rod. The marks should be exactly one inch apart. Be sure the third mark is in the center of the pencil or dowel rod.

Second, use the scissors to score, or cut, a ring around each mark on the pencil or dowel rod. The ring should go all the way around the pencil or rod. Handle the scissors carefully so that you don't cut your skin.

Next, tie a paper clip to one end of each piece of fishing line. Place each paper clip in exactly the same place on each line.

Then, thread one piece of fishing line through the hole in each bead. Each bead will rest on a paper clip.

Now, tie each piece of fishing line around the scored rings on the pencil or dowel rod. The beads must line up exactly and hang evenly.

Use one hand to hold the pencil or rod horizontally. Pull the first bead on one end back. Then release it gently. Observe what happens. The bead you release exerts a force on the other beads.

Now consider the Principle of Conservation of Energy to examine what happens to the beads on your Newton's cradle. Before you released the bead, the bead had one kind of energy called potential energy. When you let the bead fall, the potential energy changed into another kind of energy called kinetic energy. Kinetic energy is the energy of motion.

Wait. There are still more changes in energy. When the first bead hit the second bead, what did you hear? You heard a click. A click is sound energy. Now think about what happens when two things rub together. For example, if you rub your hands together, can you feel your hands getting warmer? The kinetic energy in your hands changes to heat energy. The same thing happens with the beads on your Newton's cradle. As the first bead hits the second bead, energy moves through the beads to the bead at the other end. The bead lifts, swings back, and hits the line of beads. Each time a bead hits another bead, kinetic energy changes to sound and heat energy. Eventually, the kinetic energy changes completely to sound and heat, and the beads stop moving. But don't expect this to happen quickly. The changes of energy are small, so it takes some time for the beads to stop moving.

Now you know how to build a Newton's cradle. You also know how to use the cradle to demonstrate some interesting scientific principles. Try making other Newton's cradles. Use different sizes of dowel rods and string. Change the number of beads, or use metal beads. You might even want to demonstrate your super science skills for the class.

A **Underline the correct answer that completes each statement.**

1. Sir Isaac Newton was an English
    a. artist and sculptor.
    b. principal and educator.
    c. mathematician and scientist.
    d. architect and builder.

2. A Newton's cradle demonstrates the "Principle of
    a. Conservation of Force."
    b. Conservation of Motion."
    c. Conservation of Energy."
    d. Conservation of Law."

3. The cradle shows that things stay at rest unless acted on by an
    a. underground force.
    b. outside force.
    c. overhead force.
    d. inside force.

4. Energy can change form, but the total amount of energy
    a. stays the same.
    b. grows less.
    c. grows stronger.
    d. disappears.

5. You will need one of the following to make a Newton's cradle:
    a. satin ribbon
    b. glue
    c. dowel rod
    d. stapler

6. Potential energy changes into
    a. creative energy.
    b. kinetic energy.
    c. electric energy.
    d. steam energy.

7. Sir Isaac Newton lived in the
    a. 1800s and 1900s.
    b. 1400s and 1500s.
    c. 1200s and 1300s.
    d. 1600s and 1700s.

B "A Law of Motion" is an example of a how-to paper. A how-to paper usually explains steps in a process. The steps in the process must be done in sequence in order to make sense. Number the sections of this article to form a correct sequence of events.

A Scientist at Work in the Rain Forest

_____ You have always wanted to discover a new species of plant. You decide to travel to the rain forest in Brazil to conduct a detailed search of the flora.

_____ Your assistants carefully dig up the plant specimens. They bag them and number them. The plants are gently carried back to camp.

_____ Your flight is uneventful. After reaching Brazil, you hire assistants and buy supplies.

_____ Behind the waterfall, you find several species of plants that you have never seen before. It will take you a long time to carefully catalog each species and research it.

_____ Before your flight, you must gather digging tools, cameras, books, maps, and other equipment. You must apply for permission from the Brazilian government to remove specimens from the rain forest.

_____ When you fly out over the rain forest, you are sad. You wonder what other discoveries are hiding in the jungle waiting to be found. You turn your thoughts to the new plant species in the plane's cargo hold and your journey home.

_____ You show the assistants how to use the special digging tools. You show them how to wrap the roots of any plants that you might find to prepare them for transport.

_____ Finally, you make a very exciting discovery—a waterfall! The assistants help you find a way into the cave behind the spray of water. Something interesting catches your eye.

_____ At last, you decide you have taken enough specimens. It is time to return home. The plants are packed up. Soon, you will be flying back to your own country.

Synonyms are words that mean the same or almost the same. Circle the two synonyms on each line.

1. bleached   blackened   cruel   darkened
2. veteran   beginner   experienced   ancient
3. reject   invite   discard   awake
4. detailed   show   hide   demonstrate
5. ladle   cradle   push away   hold
6. emerge   retreat   come out of   calm
7. attract   continue   reveal   sustain
8. take part in   participate   oppose   survive
9. industrious   subdued   panicked   hardworking
10. rebellion   parade   protest   celebration
11. theory   menu   degree   idea

Choose a word from below to complete each sentence. Some words may not be used.

Word Box

flora	apparatus	principle
specimen	conserve	demonstrate
species	energy	exerts
catalog	dowel	wavelength
cargo	kinetic energy	specific
---

1. An instrument or tool is an _____.

2. The plants in a location are the _____.

3. A sample from a group for scientific study is a _____.

4. A group of similar organisms is a _____.

5. A rule or law is a _____.

6. To make an organized list of items is to _____.

7. The energy of motion is _____.

8. A long, wooden rod is called a _____.

9. A load carried by a plane or a ship is called _____.

10. To show how something works is to _____.

45

E Another of Newton's laws says that "for every reaction there is an equal and opposite reaction." This could be called the law of cause and effect. It means that for every action there is a result, or consequence. Read the following how-to paper and think about causes and effects.

The Color of Light

Nearly 300 years ago in England, Sir Isaac sat by his study window on a rare, sunny day. The sunlight played over the prism, a triangular piece of glass, he held in his hand. The sparkling colored light danced on the walls of his study. He noticed that when the rays of the sun, called white light, passed through the prism, the colors of the rainbow could be seen.

This made him curious. Sir Isaac was always feeling curious. When an apple had fallen on his head, it made him wonder about the force pulling on the falling apple. This led him to his theory about *gravity*. Now he was curious about the colored light he saw emerging from the prism.

Sir Isaac knew that a current theory stated that the thickness of a prism changed the actual color of light when it passed through a prism. But, he had a different idea. Sir Isaac thought that a prism *separated* the colors already present in white light. He decided to repeat the prism experiment.

Every time Sir Isaac conducted the experiment with the prism, he saw that the resulting "rainbow" light always appeared in the same order. The colors produced—red, orange, yellow, green, blue, indigo (blue violet), and violet—always maintained the same order every time he passed white light through the prism. Sir Isaac noticed that when a second prism was used, the rainbow of colors could be changed back into white light.

Unlike sound waves, light waves do not need a substance to travel through. They can travel through the emptiness of space. Ordinary sunlight, called white light, has waves of many different lengths. Each color has its own wavelength. When white light passes through a prism, each color of light bends at a specific angle. As a result, the colors leaving the prism always keep the same order. Red is the color with the longest wavelength, so it is the top band on the rainbow. Violet has the shortest wavelength, so it is the bottom band on the rainbow.

Light passing through water or raindrops in the atmosphere can create a rainbow in the sky. The drops act like little prisms bending white light and separating it into the different colors.

Sir Isaac's theory of light and color was a new one. Many scientists of his day were angry with him. They did not agree with his theory. He eventually grew tired of the argument and wrote a letter saying he was sorry he ever put forth his idea.

Match the correct effect to its cause. Look back through the article. Write the letter of the effect beside its cause.

CAUSE	EFFECT
_____ 1. Colored light danced on Newton's study wall and	a. emerged from the prism in a rainbow of colors.
_____ 2. An apple falling made Newton wonder and	b. the colored light blended back into white light.
_____ 3. Newton noticed that white light going into a prism	c. can create a rainbow in the sky.
_____ 4. When Newton repeated the prism experiment,	d. it discouraged Newton and he wrote a letter of regret.
_____ 5. When Newton used a second prism on the rainbow light,	e. led him to his theory about the force called gravity.
_____ 6. Because red has the longest wavelength,	f. it emerges as the top band of color.
_____ 7. Because violet has the shortest wavelength,	g. he noticed the colors always kept the same order.
_____ 8. Light passing through raindrops	h. made him curious.
_____ 9. When other scientists argued with Newton's light theory,	i. it emerges as the bottom band of color.

A Read the article below. Note the details. Underline the main idea, or topic sentence, in each paragraph. Then answer the questions.

Chameleons

1.   Most chameleons live in the rain forest where the climate is warm and rainy. But, chameleons live in many different habitats all over the continent of Africa and on the island country of Madagascar just off the coast of Africa. They can even live in the dry sands of the desert or in higher elevations in the mountains.

2.   There are many different kinds of trees and plants in the rain forest that provide food and shelter for chameleons. The trees, vines, and other plants grow close together, giving the chameleon many places to hide from predators. The rain forest is ideal for chameleons.

3.   Chameleons are reptiles, or cold-blooded crawling animals. A reptile's body warms or cools to about the same temperature as the air or water around it. The mild, or temperate, moist climate of the rain forest is suited to the needs of the chameleon's body.

4.   Chameleons are also lizards, but they differ from other lizards in a few ways. Chameleons cannot grow new tails if they are injured like other lizards do. Chameleons also move more slowly than most lizards.

5.   Chameleons have bulging, heavy-lidded eyes that are unique. Chameleons can move each of their eyes in a different direction. One eye can look forward while the other looks backward. This is handy for spying and catching prey.

6.   Sunlight, temperature, and mood make some chameleons change their color. This special color-changing feature makes chameleons of interest to scientists. Scientists have found that chameleons do not use their color-changing ability to hide. It is the chameleon's normal color that provides them with camouflage.

1. What is the main idea of the sixth paragraph? Write the topic sentence.

   _____

   _____

2. Which paragraph tells some features of a chameleon's eyes? Underline the correct answer.
   a. paragraph 4   b. paragraph 5   c. paragraph 3

3. What is the main idea of paragraph 2? Underline the correct answer.
   a. The rain forest provides food and shelter.
   b. Rain forest trees give chameleons places to hide from predators.
   c. The plants of the rain forest grow close together.
   d. The rain forest is ideal for chameleons.

4. What is paragraph 4 mainly about? Underline the correct answer.
   a. Chameleons differ from other lizards.
   b. Chameleons cannot grow new tails.
   c. Chameleons are lizards.
   d. Chameleons move more slowly than other lizards.

5. Which is the best title for the whole article? Remember that the name of the story should tell what the article is mainly about. Underline the best title.
   a. Reptiles of the Rain Forest
   b. Jungle Lizards
   c. The Color of Chameleons
   d. Hidden Predators
   e. A Quick Look at Chameleons

6. Why do you think scientists might be interested in chameleons?

   _____

   _____

   _____

   _____

   _____

   _____

   _____

   _____

Read the article and write a summary of it on the lines below. Then, go back and underline the sentences in the article that represent an opinion.

What Happened to the Maya?

No one is certain about what caused the great Maya civilization to begin fading. Around A.D. 900, the Maya stopped carving the standing stones, called stelae, on which they recorded their history. There is evidence that many Maya began leaving their cities at this time. The rain forest grew over the ruins of the Mayan stone temples and buildings. It is sad that such an advanced culture is no more.

In 1238, the Maya living in the Yucatan moved their capital city from Chichen Itza to Mayapan. They built Mayapan with a thick stone wall surrounding it to protect the city from enemies. Perhaps the Maya were looking for some peace after all their troubles.

In the 1500s, the Spanish conquistadors came to Mesoamerica. They wanted to find gold and riches to take back to Spain. Gold is difficult for everyone to resist since it is so beautiful. The Spanish found about sixty Maya cities and began to conquer them. Some were taken easily. In other cities, the Maya fought in ferocious battles and repulsed the Spanish invaders.

The Maya who lived in the Yucatan peninsula refused to surrender. They fought with the Spanish for twenty years. The Spanish made some of them slaves. Others were converted to Spanish beliefs. The Spanish destroyed Mayan art and books to keep the Maya under control. Maybe the Spanish did not care for the Mayan art style. One group of Maya, the Itza, stayed free until 1697. When Mexico became its own country in 1821, the Maya tried to take back their land several times without success.

_____

_____

_____

_____

_____

_____

_____

_____

1.   The Maya civilization started around 2000 B.C. in Mesoamerica. Mesoamerica is the area covered by what is now southern Mexico, Guatemala, and parts of Belize and Honduras. The Maya built many large cities and buildings, including stone pyramids.

2.   Ancient Maya history has three main time periods. The first is called the Preclassic Period. The Preclassic Period was from 2000 B.C. to A.D. 300. Not much is known about this period of Mayan history. Archeologists believe, however, that the Maya learned to grow and irrigate crops during this time. They also began to build cities, and they developed a written language.

3.   The Classic Period lasted from about A.D. 300 to 900. Each Maya city was like its own country with its own ruling royal family. Each ruler passed the governing of the city on to the oldest son in succession. It is thought that the Maya had a population of about 10 million at this time.

4.   The Postclassic Period lasted from about A.D. 900 until the Spanish conquered the Maya in the 1600s. The Mayan cities and culture began to grow weak. Sieges between cities began over water rights and food.

Draw lines to match each paragraph to its main idea.

Paragraph 1   a. The Postclassic Period was a difficult time for the Maya.

Paragraph 2   b. The Maya civilization began in Mesoamerica.

Paragraph 3   c. In the Classic Period, rulers of cities established themselves.

Paragraph 4   d. Mayan history is divided into three time periods.

                        e. It is thought that Mayan culture began to develop in the Preclassic Period.

D   **Place the dates below in the time chart in correct order along with what happened. Then read the dates and information to learn about Mayan history.**

1821—Mexico wins independence from Spain.

980—The Toltecs conquer the Maya.

1546—The Spanish conquer the Yucatan Maya.

300—A Mayan royal ruling class develops.

1697—The last Maya city is defeated by the Spanish.

638—The great king of the Maya, Pascal, dies.

800–900—The Maya begin to leave their cities.

1502—Christopher Columbus meets Mayan traders.

700—Mayan culture is at its height.

Maya Time Chart from A.D. 300	
A.D. 300 to A.D. 900 Classic Period	
A.D. 900 to A.D. 1700 Postclassic Period	
1700 to Present	

Circle two antonyms in each group of words below.

1. ferocious   jubilant   mild   displeased
2. resist   despise   join   disable
3. discount   theory   disorder   fact
4. temptation   condense   lengthen   treat
5. camouflaged   expelled   exposed   disordered
6. unafraid   regulated   feud   uncontrolled
7. enlist   dwell   resign   enforce
8. release   exile   sieze   environment
9. actual   basic   fantasy   marsh
10. tore down   believed   upheld   overdid
11. invite   delay   unafraid   repulse

Circle two synonyms in each group of words below.

1. experiment   catalog   list   ingredient
2. emptied   irrigated   irritated   watered
3. conquered   released   took over   lacquered
4. succession   jumble   in line   shrewd
5. specific   creased   detailed   fuzzy
6. golden piece   peninsula   perishable finger of land
7. dry   moist   damp   rapids
8. stormy   temperate   desert   mild
9. ambition   siege   commanded   battle
10. society   chaos   civilization asylum
11. potential   weakness   penetrate   power

G Study the information in the table. Then, answer the questions below.

Weather in Degrees (Fahrenheit)

State	City	Yesterday	Today
Ala.	Birmingham	89/69	85/68
	Mobile	93/72	91/72
Alaska	Anchorage	57/48	61/45
	Fairbanks	56/42	56/42
Ariz.	Phoenix	101/77	101/77
	Tucson	95/69	97/72
Ark.	Little Rock	78/66	71/61
Calif.	Los Angeles	85/62	85/66
	San Francisco	73/54	81/56
Colo.	Aspen	55/37	67/37
	Denver	59/33	68/44

1. Which of the following information does this table contain?
   a. rainfall in different states
   b. high and low temperatures in different states
   c. humidity in different states
   d. the daily ozone measure

2. Based on the information in the table, the figures listed are most likely for a day in which month?
   a. September   b. January
   c. December   d. February

3. Which city has the highest temperature today?
   a. Phoenix
   b. Tucson
   c. Birmingham
   d. Los Angeles

4. In the table, which two cities have the greatest difference in temperature?
   a. Mobile and Tucson
   b. Fairbanks and Denver
   c. Phoenix and Aspen
   d. Little Rock and San Francisco

A Popular Sport

Two fast-moving sports popular with vigorous people of all ages are two kinds of skating. They are in-line skating and ice-skating. Whether skaters are on the sidewalk or on the ice, most of them can enjoy hours of fun. That is, of course, if they are limber and have the right equipment.

Skaters in both sports use equipment that is alike and different. Both kinds of skates are made for speed. Today's skates let a skater skate well all the time. Skaters can also use their skates in more than one sport. However, certain kinds of skates are made for different uses. They work best when a skater uses the right skate for the right sport. That means, for example, that a hockey player uses skates made for hockey. She can also use them to figure skate. However, in that case, she will probably skate better if she uses skates made for figure skating.

All in-line skates are made for land. So, they all have the same fundamental features. An in-line skate has a boot that is usually made from plastic. The boot is firm. It holds the skater's ankles comfortably. The boot's lining comes out so it can be washed. On the outside of the boot, there are laces, buckles, or both to fasten the boot.

Ice skates also have a boot, but this boot is made only for ice. The boot is usually made from leather. It provides support for the ankles. It is also designed to be comfortable and warm. The boot's lining is made from a material that helps air move. However, the longer the skater wears the boot, the more likely the skater's feet will perspire. Over time, this can cause a boot to deteriorate, or break down. That makes it important to wipe out the boot after each use.

Both kinds of skates have one or more objects that help the skater move. In-line skates use wheels, usually four. There are three things about the wheels that require the skater's attention. They are size, hardness, and bearings. To check the size of the wheel, the skater measures the wheel's diameter in millimeters (mm). The size of the wheel is important, because the larger it is, the faster it rolls. Most ordinary in-line skates range from approximately 72 mm to 76 mm. The size is marked on the side of the wheel.

The second important feature of the wheel is its hardness. Wheels are made from a kind of plastic. The hardness of the plastic varies and is measured in durometers. A zero durometer represents the softest plastic. One hundred durometers represent the hardest plastic. The harder the plastic, the faster the skater can go.

The last important feature of a wheel is its bearings. Bearings are fundamental to the way in-line skates work. Ball bearings are inside the hubs of the wheels. These ball bearings let the wheels roll. So, the better the ball bearings, the faster the wheels roll. Good ball bearings mean a skater will get more mileage out of his or her skates as well.

Instead of wheels, ice skates use blades. The blades are attached to the soles of the boot with a screw mount. This mount holds the blade tightly in place.

Blades are made of metal, usually stainless steel. Then they are coated with another metal, such as chrome, nickel, or aluminum. The blade is solid and has a toe pick at the front end. The toe pick lets the skater grip the ice. It also helps the skater take off. A ridge runs along the bottom of the blade. This ridge is called the "hollow." The hollow cuts the ice as the skater glides over it.

Being able to come to an abrupt stop is important to every skater. Only in-line skates have brakes. Brake pads are attached to the back of each boot. The skater stops by lifting his or her toes and pressing the brake pad to the ground.

For ice skaters, stopping is another matter. There are no brakes on ice skates. Instead, the skater uses his or her legs and feet to stop. The skater presses on the sides of his or her skates to stop.

In-line skating and ice-skating are alike in some ways and different in others. Their differences make both sports interesting to many skaters. The ways they are alike let skaters skate in both sports. For ambitious skaters with the right skates, skating is several sports in one.

What will happen next?

Think about what you have learned about in-line skating and ice-skating. Write a paragraph telling what you think the next big development in skating might be.

Underline the correct answer that completes each statement.

1. Another good title for this story is
   a. Discovery on Ice.
   b. Learning About Bearings.
   c. Two Kinds of Skating.
   d. How to Take a Fall.

2. The story is comparing
   a. leather shoes and plastic shoes.
   b. in-line skates and ice skates.
   c. winter sports and summer sports.
   d. heavy clothing and light clothing.

3. Skates work the best
   a. when they are worn for a long time.
   b. when they are worn in the winter months.
   c. when there is low humidity and less friction.
   d. when the right skate is chosen for the right sport.

4. Ice skates have a boot that is usually made of
   a. leather.   b. cloth.   c. metal.   d. rubber.

5. Instead of wheels, ice skates have
   a. bearings.   b. skis.
   c. a plastic lining.   d. blades.

6. The hardness of the wheels on in-line skates is measured in
   a. millimeters.
   b. durometers.
   c. tons.
   d. pounds per square inch.

7. The blades on ice skates are made of
   a. nickel.
   b. aluminum.
   c. stainless steel.
   d. chrome.

8. The toe pick on the blade of ice skates helps a skater
   a. choose a direction to skate in.
   b. glide like a bird over the ice.
   c. clean the ice off the toe of the boot.
   d. grip the ice.

B **Outlining is a method of organizing by making an ordered list to show how ideas are related. To outline:**

1. Use Roman numerals (I, II, III) to list the main idea groups.

2. Use capital letters (A., B., C.) to list supporting ideas.

3. Use Arabic numerals (1., 2., 3.) to list details and examples.

Use the outline below to collect research for a speech about how in-line skates and ice skates are alike and different. Use the story about skates to complete the outline.

In-line Skates and Ice Skates

I. How in-line skates and ice skates are alike.

    A. Features of the skates that are alike.

        1. Both are built for speed.

        2. _____

        3. _____

    B. Parts of the skates that are alike.

        1. _____

        2. Both have devices that help the skater move.

II. How in-line skates and ice skates are different.

    A. Features of the skates that are different.

        1. In-line skates are designed for use on land, ice skates for ice.

        2. _____

        3. _____

    B. Parts of the skates that are different.

        1. _____

        2. _____

    C. How in-line skates and ice skates stop.

        1. _____

        2. _____

59

C Compare the information in the two circle graphs below and answer the questions.

Skaters in the United States—2002

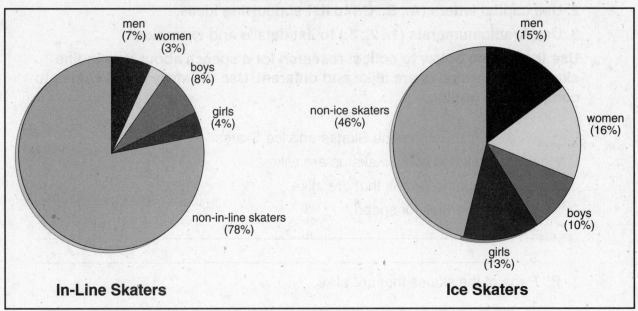

In-Line Skaters

Ice Skaters

1. What percentage of in-line skaters are men?
   a. 13 percent
   b. 7 percent
   c. 15 percent
   d. 10 percent

2. What percentage of ice skaters are women?
   a. 4 percent
   b. 20 percent
   c. 13 percent
   d. 16 percent

3. Looking at the circle graphs, which statement below is true?
   a. Fewer women ice skate than girls ice skate.
   b. More men than women in-line skate.
   c. More girls in-line skate than boys in-line skate.
   d. 18 percent of boys ice skate.

4. What percentage of ice skaters are adult males?
   a. 7 percent   b. 10 percent   c. 8 percent   d. 15 percent

5. An informal survey of skaters shows that there are more ice skaters than in-line skaters in the United States. Why do you think that is the case?

_____

D Most poets make comparisons in their work. Often the comparisons are not stated as they would be in "ordinary talk." You have to stay with the poem for a while to understand the comparisons and feel their power. Read the following poems. Then answer the questions below.

Soaring

In winter, I fly across the white horizon—
    the cold wind bites my face
    and traces my flight.
    The sound of blades slicing ice
    cuts through the splintering air.
    I'm full of graceful spins and twirls
    like a falcon turning on its wing
    high in a crisp blue sky.

Swimming

In summer, I swim along melting-hot concrete—
    the sun bounces off my helmet,
    making the world shimmer and shift.
    Wheels whine in the heat, singing
    and clicking like a dolphin.
    I jump and pump my lazy legs
    left right. left right. left right.
    through a sea of yellow hazy heat.

1. What is the poet comparing to flying like a falcon in "Soaring"?

_____

2. What is the poet comparing to swimming "along melting-hot concrete" in "Swimming"?

_____

3. What do the comparisons in "Soaring" tell you about the weather?

_____

_____

4. How does the poet compare the sound of her wheels to a dolphin in "Swimming"?

_____

5. Why do you think the world shimmers and shifts in the poem "Swimming"?

_____

E There are different ways you can compare one thing to another. Sometimes you can compare pairs of things to each other. This type of comparison is called an analogy. You need to think about how the first two things are related to each other. Then think how the next pair should be related to each other. Complete each sentence by circling the correct word.

Examples:

a. <u>Rectangle</u> is to <u>swimming pool</u> as <u>circle</u> is to <u>wheel</u>.
(A swimming pool is a rectangle, and a wheel is a circle.)

b. <u>Boot</u> is to <u>foot</u> as <u>hat</u> is to <u>head</u>.
(You wear a boot on your foot. You wear a hat on your head.)

c. <u>Artist</u> is to <u>painting</u> as <u>musician</u> is to _____. (All the words are alike because they deal with artistic activities. Which word that expresses artistic activities would fit in the comparison and make sense?)
gardening   (music)   training

1. <u>Silverware</u> is to <u>metal</u> as <u>picnicware</u> is to _____.
plastic   wood   fabric

2. <u>Freezing</u> is to <u>melting</u> as <u>uniting</u> is to _____.
joining   meeting   splintering

3. <u>Hard</u> is to <u>soft</u> as <u>stiff</u> is to _____.
asleep   limber   bored

4. <u>Singing</u> is to <u>music</u> as <u>skating</u> is to _____.
sports   cooking   ice rinks

5. <u>Bicycle chains</u> are to <u>bike wheels</u> as <u>bearings</u> are to _____.
durometers   skate wheels   ice-skate blades

6. <u>Building</u> is to <u>square footage</u> as <u>trip</u> is to _____.
inches   durometers   mileage

7. <u>Cold</u> is to <u>chills</u> as <u>heat</u> is to _____.
perspiration   exercise   thermometer

8. <u>Sadness</u> is to <u>tears</u> as <u>teasing</u> is to _____.
love   laziness   embarrassment

9. <u>Painting</u> is to <u>canvas</u> as <u>writing</u> is to _____.
paper   encyclopedia   desk

F **Find a word from below that is a synonym for the underlined word or words in each sentence. Then write each sentence using the new word.**

┌─────────────────── Word Box ───────────────────┐
│ approximate   deteriorate   ambitious   │
│ fundamentals   abruptly   limber   │
└───┘

1. The measurement was <u>close</u>, but not exact.

   _____

2. Because she is very <u>motivated,</u> she wants to make the Honor's List.

   _____

   _____

3. The green leaves fell in the pond water and began to <u>rot</u>.

   _____

4. He had missed out on the <u>basics</u> of algebra and was behind in the class.

   _____

   _____

5. She is a dancer and is very <u>flexible</u>.

   _____

G **Write all the words from below that mean the same or almost the same as vigorous.**

┌─────────────────── Word Box ───────────────────┐
│   tireless   heroic   brilliant   │
│   spirited   energetic   unfailing   │
│   gallant   panicked   strong   │
│   cowardly   strenuous   unweary   │
│   lively   talented   bashful   │
└───┘

1. _____   2. _____

3. _____   4. _____

5. _____   6. _____

7. _____   8. _____

63

A Look at Spices

Though you might find it hard to believe, people have worked and fought for spices. Among the most valued spices are salt, pepper, and saffron. You may shower your French fries with salt or sprinkle extra pepper on your hamburger. You may enjoy the color and smell of saffron rice. Chances are, you don't give these spices a second thought. Nevertheless, throughout history people have made and spent fortunes for these spices.

Let's look at ordinary table salt first. Salt is found in seawater, in salt wells, and beneath the ground. Heat energy is needed to remove salt from seawater. Large pools of water are left in the sun. Also, large pans of salt water, called dryers, may be placed over fires. Water evaporates and leaves salt behind.

A salt well is like an oil well. Two pipes, one inside the other, are drilled into the ground. Fresh water is pumped down. Salt in the soil dissolves in the water. As more fresh water is forced down, the salt water is forced up. Once it's on the surface, the water is treated like ocean water. That is, it's heated until it evaporates and leaves the salt behind.

Salt is also part of rocks almost everywhere around the world. People dig mines beneath the ground and use machines to break the rock salt apart and bring it to the surface. It is crushed to different sizes and bagged or boxed for consumers. In our hands or on our food, salt is a grainy, white substance with no scent.

Salt has a long history. Even in ancient times, people used salt for different purposes, including seasoning and preserving their food. About 3,000 B.C., Chinese people wrote about salt in their books of medicine. In ancient Egypt salt was used to preserve dead bodies. In ancient Rome soldiers were paid in salt. Some say the word *soldier* comes from the words *sal dare*, which mean to give salt. Salt was once pressed into coins more valuable than gold. Thus, people have fought wars and traveled far to find and control it.

Pepper is another important spice. Unlike salt, pepper begins as a berry. Pepper plants are shrubs that climb like vines or trail across the ground. They grow where it is hot, such as in

Indonesia. Pepper plants form small green berries about the size of a pea. As the berries ripen, they turn red. When they change color, the berries are picked, cleaned, and dried. Whether they bake in the sun or over fires, as they heat, the berries turn black. The berries are then ground to make a powder. The powder may be black, white, or red, depending on the kind of pepper plant that made the berries and the process used to make the pepper. No matter the color, pepper has a scent and sharp taste that make it easy to identify.

In the early days of trade between Europe and India, pepper was so expensive that it was reserved for royalty. A king or queen might receive a few pounds of pepper as a gift. One king, named Alaric I, is said to have demanded pepper to stop his attack on Rome in A.D. 408 Hippocrates, the father of medicine, thought pepper helped the heart and kidneys work. Even today, people use pepper as a medicine.

Saffron comes from the female parts of the purple saffron crocus, a flower. Each flower must be picked by hand in the autumn when the flowers are fully open. It may take up to 250,000 flowers to make one pound of saffron. That helps explain why saffron is one of the most expensive spices you can buy. Saffron is sold in the form of a yellow-orange powder or as slender red threads. Most of the world's saffron crocus flowers are grown in India, Iran, and Spain.

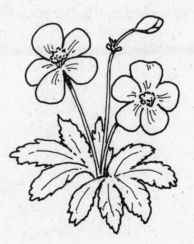

Like salt and pepper, saffron is used to season food and as medicine. In India, hosts give their guests food flavored with saffron as a sign of honor. People also use saffron to treat or prevent diseases, such as the common cold.

Records show that people in ancient Egypt and Rome around 27 B.C. used saffron as a dye for cloth. They also used it to make perfumes and medicines and to season food. Traders carried the spice through Asia, and in time, through Europe. Because the spice was expensive, people used it as a sign of their wealth and power. In the early 1500s, the ladies in the court of King Henry VIII, for example, used saffron to dye their hair.

How Spicy?

What is your favorite spice or seasoning? If you were on a desert island, what meal would you daydream about? Write a brief paragraph describing your imaginary feast.

Underline the correct answer that completes each statement.

1. The most valued spices talked about in the article are
   a. garlic, pepper, and nutmeg.
   b. saffron, cinnamon, and garlic.
   c. salt, pepper, and saffron.
   d. nutmeg, salt, and cinnamon.

2. The article says that salt is found in
   a. salt wells, seawater, and underground.
   b. rivers, ponds, and lakes.
   c. tears, salt shakers, and grocery stores.
   d. flowers, trees, and plants.

3. Heat energy is needed to remove salt from
   a. spices.
   b. pepper.
   c. seawater.
   d. saffron.

4. Chinese people wrote about salt approximately
   a. 50 years ago.   b. 5,000 years ago.
   c. 2,000 years ago.   d. 6,000 years ago.

5. Egyptians used salt to preserve
   a. jellies.
   b. dried figs.
   c. flowers.
   d. dead bodies.

6. Pepper plants are
   a. shrubs.
   b. trees.
   c. grown under water.
   d. black.

7. Saffron comes from the
   a. yellow sunflower.   b. purple crocus.
   c. red rose.   d. white daisy.

8. People in ancient Egypt and Rome used saffron as a
   a. sewing thread.
   b. cleaner.
   c. necklace.
   d. dye.

B Use the outline on page 69 to organize your thoughts for a paper you have been assigned on the history of spices. Use the short report about spices and the additional information boxes to complete the outline. Only use **relevant** information.

Additional Information Box

Mohandas K. Gandhi was a leader of the Indian struggle for independence. People called him Mahatma, which means "great soul." He believed that it is wrong to hurt another person. He thought the best way to make the British leave India was to refuse to obey unfair laws. He called this passive, or peaceful, resistance.

When the British put a tax on salt that made it too costly for poor Indians, he decided he would walk to the sea and make salt himself. He started to walk the 150 miles to the sea. Along the way, people saw what he was doing and followed him. Thousands joined him in his march to the sea. When they saw their own strength in numbers, the Indian people began to resist the British in a series of nonviolent protests. These protests succeeded in ridding India of British rule in 1947.

Ghandi's nonviolent example has influenced many people and world leaders. Dr. Martin Luther King, Jr., successfully used Ghandi's methods in the civil rights movement in the United States.

Additional Information Box

From early times spices have been treasured by many cultures. The Greeks conquered the southern Asian area in the mid-300s B.C., and the Romans had early contact with India and traded for salt and other spices.

Arab traders first began invading India in the 600s A.D.

Then the Europeans began to move into India and Indonesia. The Portugese explorer Vasco da Gama challenged Arab control of the spice trade with India in 1498. His ship was met with Indian gunfire and a blockade in an Indian harbor.

In the 1600s, Queen Elizabeth I, the sovereign of Britain, sent a group of traders to India. The British East India Company managed to gain power by signing treaties and forcing alliances with different Indian princes. The British were well-placed to gain power in India. They eventually controlled the spice trade in the 18th century.

A History of Spices

I. Three important spices

   A. Salt

      1. Found in seawater, salt wells, and under the ground

      2. A white, grainy spice with no scent

   B. _____

      1. _____

      2. White, red, or black powder

   C. Saffron

      1. _____

      2. _____

      3. _____

II. Purposes and value of spices

   A. Salt

      1. _____

      2. _____

      3. _____

      4. _____

      5. _____

   B. Pepper

      1. _____

      2. _____

   C. _____

      1. _____

      2. _____

      3. _____

      4. _____

      5. _____

      6. _____

      7. _____

III. Fighting over spices throughout history

    A. Greeks in southern Asia in the mid-300s B.C.

    B. _____

    C. The Arabs in India in 600s A.D.

    D. _____

    E. _____

        1. _____

        2. _____

        3. _____

IV. Modern people struggle over spices

    A. _____

    B. _____

    C. _____

C **Write a word from below to complete each sentence.**

Word Box		
blockade	Indonesia	seasonings
evaporates	nonviolent	spectator
exposure	preserve	sovereign

1. An area of the world south of China is _____.

2. The highest ruler in the land is a _____.

3. To be peaceful and not fight is to be _____.

4. Water that dries into the atmosphere _____.

5. Spices that add flavor to foods are called _____.

6. To keep something fresh is to _____.

7. Someone who observes or watches is a _____.

8. To be an obstacle or to stop someone from passing is to _____.

D **Choose words from below to solve the crossword puzzle.**

— **Word Box** —

expensive	sal dare	crocus
trial	pepper	opens
lesson	daisies	shrub
skate	blockades	dryers
preserves	unless	saffron
India	royalty	salt

Across

1. Roman words that mean <u>soldier</u>
3. a spice that is a powder made from dried berries
4. a small, bushy plant
6. the opposite of <u>shuts</u>
8. a boot with a blade mounted on it
10. something to be learned
11. small flowers
12. a spice that comes from seawater

Down

2. salt pans set out in the sun
5. obstacles in a road
7. a word that means <u>except</u>
9. a judge conducts this

E A **time line** is a good way to put events in the correct order. It can also be
used to organize some kinds of materials into a shorter, more readable form.
To fill out a time line, you must understand dates. Look back at the article
called "A Look at Spices" and the Additional Information boxes about the
history of salt. Find all the dates mentioned and place them on the time line
below. Start with the earliest date at the top of the line and continue adding
dates in order until the latest date is at the bottom end of the line. Add the
information about what happened.

The History of Spices—Time Line

The Mystery of the Singing Bat

One day in December 1994, Barbara French began her daily routine. You might be surprised to learn what kind of routine she keeps. She takes care of bats. Barbara's bats are Mexican free-tailed bats (*Tadarida brasiliensis*). The bats she cares for have been hurt and cannot return to the wild. Barbara thought this December day would be like any other, but it wasn't. She got a real surprise. The surprise was the beginning of a scientific discovery.

As Barbara fed the bats, she heard an unfamiliar, bird-like song. She stopped to listen. She heard all of the normal sounds. She recognized Hannah's buzz. Hannah buzzes when she defends her favorite roosting spot. Then Barbara heard Wheatley's squeal. She could tell that another bat had chased him away from the mealworm tray. Barbara also heard the chirp Amy makes when she wants to be fed by hand. But she had never heard this new song before.

Barbara decided to solve the mystery. Whenever she heard the song, Barbara popped her head into the bat cage. As soon as her head was inside the cage, the singing stopped. It took Barbara two weeks to find the singing bat. The singer was Hank, an adult male. He seemed to be singing to a small group of females in his roosting pocket. A roosting pocket is a handmade fabric pouch, or bag, in the bats' cage.

In the following weeks, the male bats became unusually bold and ready to fight. They chased each other all the time. Free-tailed bats usually like the company of other bats, so Barbara thought this behavior was odd. Ordinarily, the bats like to roost together.

Barbara was worried by this change in the bats' behavior. Her familiar little bat colony was suddenly very different. The bats had been happy with each other for the past year. Of course, they sometimes squabbled, pushed, shoved, and swatted at each other. However, these were normal bat behaviors. Plus, the bats always settled their differences quickly. They didn't hurt each other. The bat that started a fight usually tried to end the fight. He or she would snuggle up with the other bats. It was as if the bat wanted to say it was sorry. The entire colony seemed to work together to keep the peace. However, Hank was different.

One day Barbara watched Hank attack Joshua, another bat. Hank darted from his pocket. He buzzed loudly and chased Joshua around the cage. Barbara decided Joshua had probably moved too near Hank's territory. Before Barbara could stop him, Hank caught Joshua and snagged his ear. Hank's anger bothered Barbara, but what followed really upset her. Moments after she had rescued Joshua, he squeezed out of her hand. Joshua zoomed off, making an excursion into Hank's territory. Joshua seemed ready to fight back.

Because she didn't understand the bats' new behaviors, Barbara decided to ask for help. She called Amanda Lollar. Amanda is a licensed expert in the care of captive Mexican free-tailed bats. Amanda told Barbara that Hank was probably "singing to his women." Amanda also told Barbara to watch for pups that would probably be born during the summer. Barbara was surprised that the explanation was so simple. The bats that Barbara cared for would never be wild again. Their problems made it impossible for them to care for themselves. Barbara didn't think that the bats were strong enough to have healthy pups.

The problems were not over. Barbara and the other bats found Hank's behavior too hard to manage. Hank fought with other males all the time. He bit Joshua's ear again. He even tried to attack Barbara as she fed a female.

Barbara noticed something new. Three females that had been roosting with Hank suddenly began eating more. They ate everything Barbara fed them and wanted more.

Finally, Hank's singing stopped. The females left Hank and moved into Wheatley's roosting area. Eventually, Hank became himself again. The Hank problem was solved, but a Wheatley problem began. Wheatley began to guard the females that were expecting babies. Wheatley became as fierce as Hank had been.

In June, as Barbara was feeding the bats, she saw a little, pink pup about the size of a walnut. Although the baby was very young, he was able to follow his mother around inside the roosting pocket. Twelve days later, Barbara saw the birth of a second pup. This baby was born with his eyes open. He was able to lick his tiny wings clean within minutes after birth. Barbara learned a lot from her experience with her bats. So did scientists who study bats. Barbara was able to give scientists information they had never had before. Hank's music wasn't a mystery anymore. Neither was Wheatley's protective behavior. Thanks to Barbara and her bats, scientists now know much more about the mating behaviors of Mexican free-tailed bats.

Why make observations?

How do you think Barbara's observations contributed to scientific knowledge? Write a short paragraph telling what other animal researchers might learn from her discoveries.

A **Underline the correct answer for each question.**

1. What type of story is this?
   a. It is a movie review.
   b. It is a true story.
   c. It is a fairy tale.
   d. It is a how-to paper.

2. What does Barbara French work with?
   a. fruit bats   b. wombats
   c. Mexican free-tailed bats   d. vampire bats

3. What did Barbara hear that caught her attention?
   a. a squeal   b. a buzz
   c. a chirp   d. a bird-like song

4. Who was responsible for the unusual sound in the cage?
   a. Hank   b. Hannah
   c. Amy   d. Joshua

5. What is a roosting pocket?
   a. a pouch on the mother bat
   b. a handmade fabric pouch
   c. a cardboard box
   d. a wooden perch

6. Why did Barbara call Amanda Lollar?
   a. She wanted a partner for a new scientific study.
   b. She wanted to catch up on what Amanda had been doing.
   c. She needed expert help to understand the bat's new behavior.
   d. She wanted to ask her for a ride to the science fair.

7. What did Amanda say was happening?
   a. Amy was "talking in her sleep."
   b. Hank was "singing to his women."
   c. Hannah was "chattering."
   d. Joshua was "whistling a tune."

8. What did the three females start doing?
   a. eating less
   b. flying upside down
   c. eating more
   d. scratching on the walls of the cage

B Write a summary on the lines below of the short report called "The Mystery of the Singing Bat." Remember, a summary is a brief restatement of the main points of a paragraph or article.

_____

_____

_____

_____

_____

_____

_____

_____

_____

_____

_____

_____

Read the following article about bats. In each paragraph, write M on the line before the sentence that contains the main idea. Before supporting details, write SD. Before slightly related facts, write SR.

Bats

1. _____ Bats sleep during the day and hunt for food at night. _____ They are nocturnal. _____ Most bats are insectivores, or eat insects. _____ Bats help keep the insect population under control. _____ One small bat can eat up to 600 mosquitoes, moths, or other insects in an hour. _____ In Texas, there are about 20 million bats living in Braken Cave. _____ They are Mexican free-tailed bats, and they eat about 200 tons of insects every night. _____ Some kinds of bats eat fish, frogs, birds, scorpions, and mice. _____ Some eat fruits and plants.

2. _____ There are also bats that eat pollen and nectar. _____ Nectar is a sweet liquid found inside a plant or flower. _____ Some bats have long noses that they can push down into the center of flowers to find nectar and pollen. _____ Bats are important because they are pollinators for many plants, including bananas. _____ Pollinators are animals that spread pollen. _____ Pollen is a dusty substance that fertilizes plants.

3. _____ Most fruit-eating bats cannot digest seeds in the fruit they eat. _____ The seeds leave the bats' bodies in the form of waste. _____ Waste is undigested food that leaves an animal's body in droppings. _____ Some of the seeds grow into new fruit trees.

4. _____ Bat waste is called guano. _____ Guano provides fertilizer for growing crops. _____ Many people around the world use guano to make the soil healthy and full of nutrients that are good for growing plants.

5. _____ There are almost 1,000 species of bats. _____ Bats are divided into two main groups called megabats and microbats.

_____ Megabats are very large, and microbats are small.

_____ Most bats fall into the microbats category. _____ Most microbats weigh less than 2 ounces (56.7 grams). _____ The smallest microbat is a bumblebee bat, which is found in Thailand. _____ It is the size of a fingernail and weighs less than a dime.

6. _____ There are nearly 200 species of megabats. _____ Flying foxes are the largest of all the megabats. _____ They can weigh up to 4 pounds (1.8 kg) and have wingspans up to 6 feet (1.8 m).

7. _____ Some bats have spots or other color patterns on their wings. _____ Colors, shapes, and patterns help the bats blend in with their habitat. _____ This is called camouflage. _____ Camouflage makes it difficult for the bat's enemies to see them. _____ Speckled bats can blend in with an environment that is made up of bark or rocks. _____ Red, orange, and gold bats can hide in fruit trees and look like ripe fruit.

8. _____ Bats have unusual features that set them apart from other animals. _____ One bat, the leaf-nosed bat, has a nose with flaps of skin that look like leaves. _____ Bats have tails of different lengths. _____ The tails of some bats are short. _____ Other bats have tails that stick out past their legs. _____ Some bats are tailless._____ The wings of bats are covered by a thin tissue of skin called a membrane. _____ Each wing has four long fingers and one thumb with a claw. _____ A bat's wings are attached to its hind legs, and the membrane stretches behind the legs.

9. _____ While hunting food at night, bats make a series of high-pitched sounds that are too high for people to hear. _____ When the sounds hit an object, they bounce back to the bat's ears. _____ This is also how an echo works. _____ Bats use the sounds to find and catch flying insects in the dark. _____ The ability to use echoes to locate objects is called echolocation.

Choose a word from below to complete each sentence. Some words may not be used.

┌─────────────────────────── **Word Box** ───────────────────────────┐

compete	roosting	nocturnal
squabble	pollinators	nectar
environment	echolocation	insectivores
territory	membrane	undigested
excursion	licensed	fertilizer

└──┘

1. Animals that spread pollen are _____.

2. Bats resting on their perch or in their pouches are _____.

3. To struggle against another for something is to _____.

4. Bouncing sound off objects to locate them is called _____.

5. A very thin piece of skin is a _____.

6. Animals that are active at night are _____.

7. Bat guano that is used to improve soil is called _____.

8. A trip is an _____.

9. To have little arguments is to _____.

10. Your surroundings are your _____.

From the article called "Bats," list four positive things that bats do for people and the environment. Use a word from the word list above in each of your four answers.

_____

_____

_____

_____

_____

_____

_____

_____

E A **hypothesis** is a guess that is made to explain a certain event or fact until the actual cause can be proved. Scientists Barbara French and Amanda Lollar had a hypothesis about why Hank was "singing." They used their hypothesis, or guess, until they could prove what was true. Read each of the following paragraphs. Write a hypothesis to explain what you think is happening in each paragraph. Then, write what you would do to prove your hypothesis.

1. Snow has covered the ground, and the temperature has been below freezing for days. However, this morning you awake to find puddles all over the sidewalk. The icicles along your roofline are dripping.

Hypothesis: _____

_____

What could you do to prove your hypothesis? _____

_____

_____

2. You think you feel the floor shaking. Then, books on the shelves begin to fall over. Glasses in the kitchen cabinets are clinking. You notice the chandelier over the dining table is swinging. Pictures begin to fall off the walls.

Hypothesis: _____

_____

What could you do to prove your hypothesis? _____

_____

_____

3. You and a friend go to a pond. You each find a frog to enter in the local frog jumping race. When you bring the frogs back home, you let them out of their boxes. Your friend's frog hops away quickly. Your frog takes one slow hop and then quits.

Hypothesis: _____

_____

What could you do to prove your hypothesis? _____

_____

_____

_____

F Observation is very important trait for scientists and learners of all kinds. Look at the two graphics below, read the labels, and compare the structure of a human ear to a bat ear. In one list, write down the likenesses you see. In the second list, write the differences you observe.

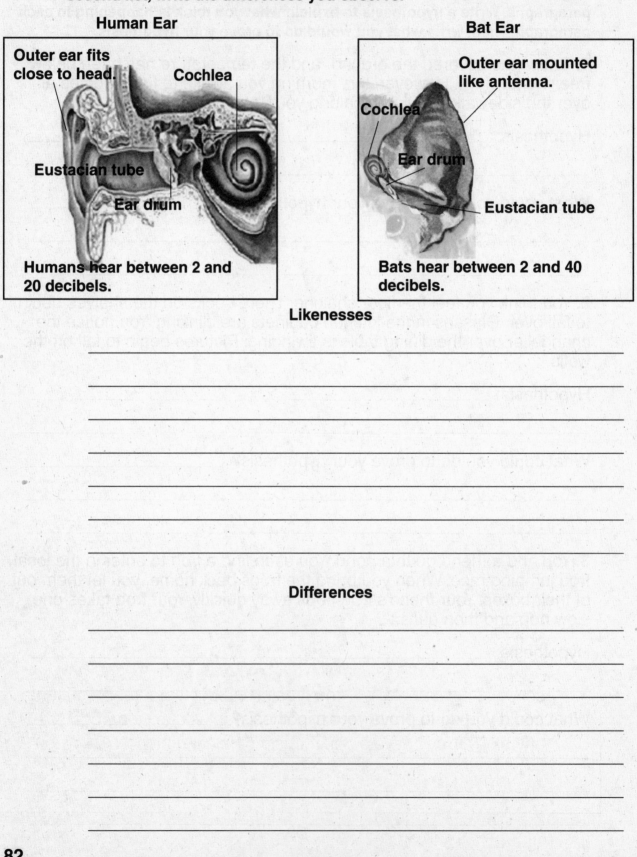

Human Ear

Outer ear fits close to head.

Cochlea

Eustacian tube

Ear drum

Humans hear between 2 and 20 decibels.

Bat Ear

Outer ear mounted like antenna.

Cochlea

Ear drum

Eustacian tube

Bats hear between 2 and 40 decibels.

Likenesses

_____

_____

_____

_____

_____

_____

Differences

_____

_____

_____

_____

_____

_____

121 Sparrow Lane
Mason City, Iowa
November 12, 2003

Carlos Gonzales
P.O. Box 122
Des Moines, Iowa

Dear Carlos,

Everyone here is fine and looking forward to the Thanksgiving holiday. School is really hard. All of us at school are going nuts. Even Mom and Dad are ready for a break. We can't wait for the holiday. I just wish you were going to be here to share it with us.

Mom said that you called Thursday night while I was at play practice. Did I tell you that I got the lead in the school play? It's pretty good, I guess. Anyway, I'm sorry that I didn't get to talk to you. Maybe I could have convinced you to come home for Thanksgiving. Mom said that you're going home with your roommate. Where is Aspen, Colorado, anyway?

Everyone will be here—Abuelita, Abuelito, Uncle Eduardo, Aunt Anna, Michael, Mom, Dad, and of course, me. Everybody will be here but you. I don't know if you've thought much about Abuelito lately. He's getting old, you know. Nanny told Mom that the last time Aunt Anna visited, Abuelito couldn't remember her name. I bet he'd remember you, though. Abuelito always really loved you. Thanksgiving would be a perfect time to see him, don't you agree?

It's been awhile since we've talked. Since you went away to school, I haven't had anyone to talk to about those really personal things. You know what I mean. I don't want you to worry or anything. I don't have a big, horrible problem right now. But you never know when one's going to come up, and then what will I do? We've never talked about how to handle personal emergencies while you're away. It sure seems like Thanksgiving would be a perfect time to talk about that.

Oh, I just thought of another reason you should come home for Thanksgiving. I have two words for you—football game. How can we have our traditional family game if you aren't here? We don't have enough players without you. Do you remember last year when I made that extra point just seconds before we were called into dinner? I think that was the best Thanksgiving game we've ever had, don't you? I wonder. Does your roommate's family play football on Thanksgiving? I hope you will tell him how much fun we all have playing together. Tell him if he joins us, we'll take it easy on him! Does your roommate know that you led your high school team to the district playoffs last year? Here is a drawing I did for you:

I think I've almost run out of things to say. Wait, I remember one other thing. Mrs. Sanchez visited the other day. I heard her tell Mom that Marcie was coming home for Thanksgiving. Wow. I haven't seen Marcie since you and she took me camping right before school started. Remember how beautiful the stars were? And it was so much fun singing all the old songs together. That was a great time. Just thinking about it makes me want to go camping again. I wonder if Marcie would like to put up a tent in the backyard. We could have Thanksgiving dinner out there. Of course, camping might not be as much fun if it's just the two of us. It wouldn't feel right without you.

Well, Carlos, I think I'm at the end of this letter. I don't know what else to write. I sure would like to see you at Thanksgiving. It won't be the same if you're not here. Of course, I'm not trying to pressure you. It's your decision. I know you'll do the right thing. Besides, you're probably not as crazy about Abuelita's famous homemade cranberry sauce as I am. And I can't remember if lemon icebox pie is still your favorite dessert. I'm making one, you know. There's going to be a lot of really good food. Turkey and a special salsa dressing, Mama's special spicy beans, Tia's sweet potatoes, and much, much more. Oh, well. I bet the food in Aspen is pretty good, too. I really am going to say goodbye now. I sure miss you. I will be thinking about you over the holiday. I hope you have a great Thanksgiving. I'll do the best I can without you.

Your best and only sister,

Daniella

P.S. Does your roommate like lemon icebox pie? I can make a pumpkin pie if he likes that better.

Underline the correct answer to each question.

1. What is Daniella's purpose for writing the letter?
   a. She wants Carlos to take her to the autumn dance.
   b. She wants to tell Carlos how much she cares for him.
   c. She wants Carlos to come home for the holiday.
   d. She wants to join Carlos in Aspen for the holiday.

2. What holiday does the letter refer to?
   a. Christmas
   b. Halloween
   c. Ramadan
   d. Thanksgiving

3. Why does Daniella ask questions about Carlos's roommate's likes and dislikes?
   a. She has a crush on the roommate.
   b. She hopes to interest the roommate in joining them for the holiday.
   c. She is showing polite interest in the roommate's feelings.
   d. She hopes to hide her dislike for the roommate by asking about him.

4. What food does Daniella tempt Carlos with?
   a. pumpkin pie
   b. mincemeat pie
   c. pecan pie
   d. lemon icebox pie

5. Who did Carlos and Daniella camp with on another occasion?
   a. Marcie
   b. Marie
   c. Mary Ellen
   d. Martha

6. What are two arguments Daniella uses to achieve her goal with Carlos?
   a. a personal problem; the homecoming parade
   b. Abuelito is old; the family football game
   c. a school dance; camping with Marie
   d. a job possibility for Carlos; their mother is ill

7. How does Daniella's closing about being his "only sister" reinforce her purpose?
   a. She tries to make him feel older.
   b. She tries to make him feel like he should invite her to Aspen.
   c. She tries to make him feel unneeded.
   d. She tries to work on any guilt Carlos might feel about not coming home.

8. What word would you use to describe the tone of Daniella's letter?
   a. coaxing
   b. angry
   c. pouting
   d. giggly

B Daniella's letter was sent through the post office. This is called "snail mail" on the Internet because it is slow. Writing e-mail letters on the Internet is a good way to stay in touch with family and friends. E-mail letters can be sent and received in a matter of minutes. Read the following short piece to learn about good manners, called "netiquette," on the Internet, or the Net. Then, answer the questions below.

Netiquette

If you are connected and sending and receiving e-mail over the Internet, you'll want to watch your "netiquette." That is the Internet way of saying, "Watch your manners and be thoughtful of others."

You'll want to practice good manners on the Internet because if you don't, you may find that no one will want to talk to you online. Some online services and ISPs (Internet Service Providers) have rules about behavior. The Internet Service Provider is the electronic link between your computer and the Internet. You may find yourself thrown off the Internet if you don't mind your manners!

When typing your e-mail, avoid using all caps. TYPING IN CAPS means you are shouting. So, please, hold down your voice and keep your finger off the "Caps lock" key.

Don't use bad language. When you are online, you may be tempted to use words that you would not use in person. But resist! Not only will people avoid you, but you could get banned by your Internet service.

Don't flame and don't be a bother. When someone behaves badly online or types angrily, it's called "flaming." Constantly bothering someone is called "harassing." You'll lose friends and get kicked off the Internet, or be charged a fine if you do either of these.

1. What does "netiquette" mean?

_____

2. Why practice netiquette?

_____

3. What does an ISP do?

_____

_____

4. What does typing in all capital letters mean?

_____

5. What is "flaming"? What does "harassing" mean?

_____

_____

C Some words have more than one meaning and pronunciation. Study the word below and its meanings. Then write the letter of the correct meaning of the word next to each sentence.

reject: a. (rē´ jĕct) *n*: An object that is damaged and cast off.

b. (rĕ jĕct´) *v*: To throw away or refuse to agree to.

<table>
<tr><td>The vase is a reject because it is cracked.</td><td>The judge will reject the vote results if they are not submitted on time.</td></tr>
</table>

_____ 1. They *reject* the idea because they do not agree with it.

_____ 2. Sam's clay pot was a *reject* because it had a chip.

_____ 3. Carlos *rejected* Daniella's arguments because they were slanted.

_____ 4. The factory line came to a stop as the *reject*, a flawed toy, was removed.

_____ 5. The shoes were scuffed and heelless, *rejects* to be thrown on the garbage pile.

_____ 6. Damian is a poor sport and *rejects* any offer of apology.

_____ 7. Daniella thought her pumpkin pie was a *reject* because it tasted so bad.

_____ 8. Carlos's abuelito *rejects* any offer of apology.

A Read the article and underline the main idea or topic sentence in each paragraph.

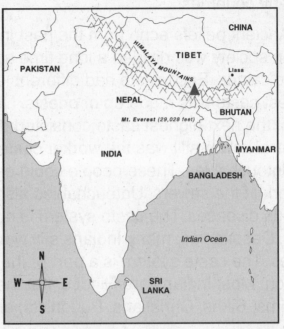

India is more crowded than almost anywhere else on Earth. Only China is more crowded. One person in every six people on the planet lives in India!

About one-third the size of the United States, India is the seventh largest country in the world in area. It is also called a subcontinent. That means it is a large land mass that is separate from, but still a part of, the continent of Asia. In fact, India takes up most of southern Asia.

The tip of India juts out into the Indian Ocean. In the north, India is separated from Nepal, China, and Tibet by the Himalayan Mountains. Pakistan, formerly a part of India, borders India to the northwest. To the east are Bangladesh and Myanmar, formerly Burma. The island country of Sri Lanka, formerly Ceylon, is just off India's southern tip. Politically and geographically, India is in a very important location.

For thousands of years, attacks, invasions, and migrations by foreigners have added to the interesting mix of people in India. Today, many groups still practice their ancient traditions. They speak their own languages. If you were to travel across India, you would hear more than two hundred different languages spoken. About seventeen of these are recognized by the Indian government. The main language of India is Hindi (HIN-dee). It is spoken by about one-third of the people. India is a country of contrasts, and some people have described it as the "country that is many countries."

Ancient beliefs echo from the past into modern India. The Indian society was divided a long time ago into groups of people, called castes. Each caste had different jobs and importance. The highest caste was made up of priests. Next came the princes. Then, the next highest caste consisted of businesspeople and farmers. Lower still was the worker caste. In the lowest caste were the untouchables. These people could only be garbage collectors or work in the sewers. Untouchables also included people with serious diseases. The caste system is now against the law in India. Despite this, many Indians still work and marry within castes. The caste system is a part of the teachings of the Hindu religion. Most Indians are Hindus, but there are also many Muslims, Sikhs, Christians, Buddhists, and Jains.

Asian-Indians have come to the United States in two major periods. The early phase of Asian-Indian movement, or migration, began around 1900 and lasted only until 1917. Six or seven thousand men from India's Punjab region made up that first small migration. They came to California in search of adventure, land, jobs, and freedom. They came from rural areas and were mainly uneducated.

The later phase of migration began after 1965, when the Immigration Act was passed. This law gave special treatment to immigrants with needed skills. After 1965, Asian-Indians immigrating to America came from all over India. They had higher educational backgrounds than the earlier immigrants. They looked to America's great cities to find their fortune. As a result, most settled in Los Angeles, California; New York, New York; Independence Town, New Jersey; and Houston, Texas.

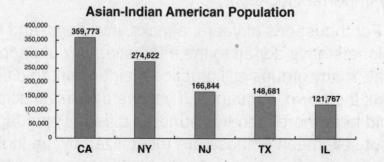

Asian-Indian American Population

State	Population
CA	359,773
NY	274,622
NJ	166,844
TX	148,681
IL	121,767

Underline the correct answer to each question.

1. In a list of largest countries, what number is India in terms of land area?
   a. tenth
   b. third
   c. second
   d. seventh

2. In a list of countries with the highest population, what number is India?
   a. second
   b. first
   c. seventh
   d. third

3. What country borders India on the northwest?
   a. Sri Lanka
   b. Pakistan
   c. Bangladesh
   d. Myanmar

4. How many languages are recognized by the Indian government?
   a. one hundred
   b. sixteen
   c. seventeen
   d. over one hundred

5. What is the main language of India?
   a. English
   b. Hindi
   c. Navajo
   d. Arabic

6. What term was used to describe the groups of people in Indian society?
   a. organizations
   b. clubs
   c. communities
   d. castes

7. What was the lowest group in India?
   a. businesspeople
   b. priests
   c. untouchables
   d. princes

8. In what U.S. state do most Indian-Americans live?
   a. California
   b. Illinois
   c. New York
   d. New Jersey

Complete the outline below using the article on India.

India and Immigration

I. The Country of India

   A. Size and Description

      1. _____

      2. _____

      3. _____

      4. _____

   B. Location and Surrounding Countries

      1. _____

      2. _____

      3. _____

      4. _____

      5. _____

      6. _____

   C. The People and Languages of India

      1. _____

      2. _____

      3. _____

II. Ancient Beliefs

   A. The Caste System

      1. _____

      2. _____

      3. _____

      4. _____

      5. _____

B. Religious Beliefs

1. _____

2. _____

3. _____

4. _____

5. _____

6. _____

III. Asian-Indian Immigrants

A. The Early Punjab Immigrants (1900–1917)

1. _____

2. _____

3. _____

4. _____

B. Asian-Indian Immigrants (after 1965)

1. _____

2. _____

3. Settled in American Cities

a. _____

b. _____

c. _____

d. _____

D **Choose a word from below to complete each sentence. Some words may not be used.**

┌─────────────────────── **Word Box** ───────────────────────┐

migration	caste	traditions
politically	contrasts	sewer
immigrants	invasions	Hindi
foreigner	persist	treatment
census	trek	priests

└───┘

1. People from other countries who come to live in the United States are called

   _____.

2. Customs of a country or ethnic group are _____.

3. A Hindu division of people is called a _____.

4. Male representatives of a religion may be called _____.

5. A count of people in a country is called a _____.

6. An underground system for getting rid of waste is a _____.

7. The main language of India is _____.

8. A movement of people or animals from one place to another is called a

   _____.

9. Strong differences are _____.

10. Attacks on a country by outside people are _____.

E Use the circle graph to answer the questions.

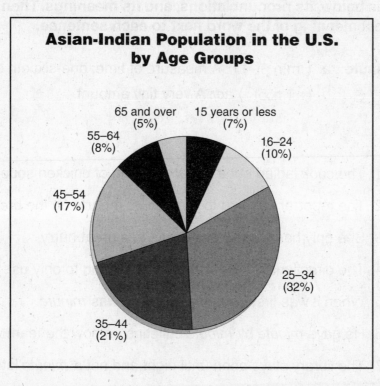

Asian-Indian Population in the U.S. by Age Groups

- 65 and over (5%)
- 15 years or less (7%)
- 55–64 (8%)
- 16–24 (10%)
- 45–54 (17%)
- 25–34 (32%)
- 35–44 (21%)

1. What percentage of the Asian-Indian people born in the United States are 65 and over?

   a. 10 percent

   b. 17 percent

   c. 5 percent

   d. 8 percent

2. What percentage of the Asian-Indian people born in the United States are age 16 to 24?

   a. 17 percent

   b. 10 percent

   c. 28 percent

   d. 8 percent

3. Looking at the circle graph, which statement below is true?

   a. Most Asian-Indian people born in the U.S. are teenagers.

   b. Most Asian-Indian people born in the U.S. are over the age of 65.

   c. Most Asian-Indian people born in the U.S. are female.

   d. Most Asian-Indian people born in the U.S. are under the age of 54.

4. What is the largest Asian-Indian age group in the U.S.?

   a. 35–44   b. 45–54   c. 55–64   d. 25–34

Some words have more than one meaning and pronunciation. Study each of the words below, its pronunciations, and its meanings. Then write the letter of the correct meaning of the word next to each sentence.

minute: a. (mĭn´ ĭt) *n*: A measure of time; one-sixtieth of an hour.

   b. (mī nōot´) *adj*: A very tiny amount.

_____ 1. The cook ladled out a *minute* serving of chicken soup.

_____ 2. The reporter gave up to the *minute* reports on the breaking news.

_____ 3. She only had a *minute* and was in a great hurry.

_____ 4. The directions on the shampoo label said to only use a *minute* amount.

_____ 5. When it was first born, the baby bat was *minute*.

_____ 6. He gave *minute* by *minute* bulletins on how the team was doing.

_____ 7. The library stays open until eight and not a *minute* later.

_____ 8. Her stitches are *minute* because she is an excellent quilter.

sewer: a. (sō´ ər) *n*: A person who sews fabric or seeds.

   b. (sōo´ ər) *n*: An underground drainage system for waste.

_____ 9. They flushed out the *sewer* with fresh water.

_____ 10. The *sewer* worked all night to finish the costume.

_____ 11. The ancient Romans were the first to design and build *sewers*.

_____ 12. The Acme sewing machine at the factory replaced all the human *sewers*.

_____ 13. In early times, *sewers* planted whole fields of wheat by hand.

_____ 14. The quilting circle has many long-time *sewers*.

_____ 15. A popular myth says that alligators live in the *sewers*.

_____ 16. The workman fell into the *sewer* and had to be rescued.

A Movie to Remember!

If a story needs one hero, one princess in distress, and one villain, or evil force, to be a fairy tale, then *Bernie, the Laughing Ogre* may be one of the funniest fairy tales you've ever seen. That's right, the word is seen, not heard. Because *Bernie, the Laughing Ogre* is a movie, and its characters are unlike any fairy tale characters you've ever met before.

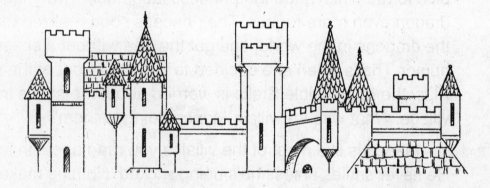

Let's start with the hero, Bernie. Bernie is tall, but definitely not handsome. In fact, he's a chubby, purple giant with too much hair. Most of the time, too much hair on a giant isn't a problem. But Bernie's hair grows in all the wrong places. There's hair between his toes and fingers. There's even hair growing from his nose and ears, but there's no hair on his head or body. Bernie is bald.

There's something else that makes Bernie a pleasant, but uncommon, hero. He's ticklish. A single scratch on his bald, purple skin makes Bernie lose control. He falls to the ground, laughing and gasping for air. Bernie knows this is unacceptable behavior for a giant. In fact, his giant friends have threatened to kick Bernie out of their drama club if he can't be more serious. Bernie wants to act like other giants, but he can't help himself.

To be safe, Bernie never goes into the nearby village where he might rub up against the moles. That may not seem so funny, but you need to remember that moles are hairy and blind. They use their whiskers to see. Their short, stubby whiskers are always moving about. If you're a bald, ticklish giant like Bernie, you can see why moles might be a problem. In fact, Bernie avoids moles altogether. That includes princess moles.

The princess in this story is no ordinary fairy-tale princess. For one thing, she's a mole. For the second thing, she's not really in distress. She's used to the dull, dark castle where she lives. She's also used to the boring dragon that holds her captive. Princess Stella has learned to make herself laugh, but only when the dragon isn't around. Nothing makes the dragon angrier than laughter. The first time the princess laughed, the dragon shook and shivered. Steam came from his ears. His skin turned from blue to red. This made the princess laugh, too. That made the dragon even more furious. The princess soon realized that of all the dragons in the world, she got the one without a sense of humor. That's when she decided to find a way out of the castle. Plus, the responsible Stella is worried about the moles in her village. What was the villain Manco doing to them?

Manco is like most of the villains you read about in fairy tales. He never smiles unless he's being wicked. Nothing makes him happier than making someone else unhappy. That's why he let the dragon into the village to kidnap the princess. He knew that once the princess was gone, everyone in the village would be sad. That's where Bernie's problem begins.

Most of the time, no one comes near the dark, unfriendly forest where Bernie lives. Until the moles come, that is. You see, some of the moles decide they need a giant to help them rescue their princess and bring laughter back to the village. Their first stop is Bernie's forest.

Unless Bernie is merciful and agrees to help, the moles tell him more moles will come. Bernie has no choice. He must say yes or risk becoming the laughingstock of giants everywhere. So, Bernie agrees to rescue the princess if the moles promise to return home. The moles promise, but that's not exactly what happens. I could tell you more, but I don't want to spoil the surprises that fill this movie. Don't think about how Bernie helps all of those hairy, whiskered moles rescue the princess. Don't imagine what the dragon does the first time he hears Bernie laugh. You'll see how the truthful Bernie handles these problems when you see the movie. Right now, I'd like to talk about something else that's going to make you love this fairy tale.

Bernie, the Laughing Ogre, the movie, is a unique example of the best of computer technology. The people who brought these characters to life have done something extraordinary. Each character walks, talks, and looks like a real living thing. When Bernie smiles, you see wrinkles in his bald skin. When the wind blows, you see each mole whisker twitch. When the dragon breathes fire, you almost feel the flames. Characters look so real, you're sure they are. The beautifully picturesque landscape is fantastic, too.

There are hundreds of wonderful reasons why you should see *Bernie, the Laughing Ogre*. There's not a single reason not to see it. This story isn't like the fairy tales you read when you were a child. It will make you laugh. You'll also be amazed by the computer graphics that made this movie. See this upbeat movie now. Then you can make plans to see it a second time because I'm sure you will.

Would you buy a ticket?

Did this review of the movie make you want to see Bernie, the Laughing Ogre? Write a short paragraph telling why the review did or did not make you want to see the movie. Include specific details from the review.

Underline the correct answer to each question.

1. What is the author's purpose in writing this movie review?
   a. to teach the reader about ogres
   b. to warn the reader about the movie
   c. to convince the reader to see the movie
   d. to tell the reader about computer graphics

2. Why does the reviewer tell the reader so much about the movie's characters?
   a. He wants to prepare the reader for disappointment.
   b. He wants to spoil the movie for his readers.
   c. He thinks the characters are badly drawn.
   d. He thinks the characters make the movie.

3. Why does the reviewer say Bernie the Ogre avoids moles?
   a. He thinks they will attack him.
   b. He thinks their eyes look scary.
   c. He is afraid the moles' whiskers will tickle him.
   d. He is afraid he will accidentally hurt the moles.

4. What are two settings mentioned in the review?
   a. a village; a dark forest
   b. a dragon's cave; a high mountaintop
   c. a sandy beach; a river bank
   d. the center of the earth; an erupting volcano

5. How did the princess become captive in the dragon's castle?
   a. Manco let the dragon kidnap her.
   b. She wandered in one day.
   c. Bernie invited the princess to visit the castle.
   d. The princess dropped in from the sky.

6. What is another good title for this review?
   a. Bernie Isn't Worth the Journey
   b. A Magical Evening at the Movies
   c. You Be the Judge!
   d. Computer Graphics: Why They Ruin a Movie

7. Why does the reviewer tell you about the computer graphics?
   a. He likes to show off.   b. He wants to educate the audience.
   c. He loves technology.   d. He thinks they are amazing.

8. Why doesn't the reviewer tell you how the movie ends?
   a. He wants his readers to guess the ending.
   b. He wants his readers to buy a ticket.
   c. He wants his readers to go see the movie.
   d. He wants his readers to make up their own ending.

B *Bernie, the Laughing Ogre* is a fantasy story, or "fairy story." Some fairy stories and fables are very old. Early people used these stories to explain things they did not understand. Here are some stories from different lands. Write the fact of nature under the story on the line provided.

Facts of Nature

what rainbows were
how the sun and the moon came to be
how day and night came about
how a river was formed
how two mountain ranges formed
what thunder was

---

1. In Irish fairy stories, little people called leprechauns hide from humans. If a lucky person can catch one of the little people, that leprechaun has to give the person a pot of gold. A leprechaun hides his gold at the end of a colorful, magic road. What do you think these Irish fairy stories tried to explain?

_____

2. In a popular American story, a man exploring a forest is startled by a loud sound. He hears the sound of rolling and then a loud crash. This happens over and over. When he explores where the sound is coming from, he finds dwarves bowling deep in the woods. What do you think this fairy story tried to explain?

_____

3. In an English fairy story, two giants live on a flat plain. They begin to quarrel and start throwing huge boulders at each other. Soon, each giant is surrounded by piles of rocks that reach the sky. What do you think this fairy story tried to explain?

_____

C **Bernie, the Laughing Ogre** is a character-driven story. That means that the characters' feelings and traits influence the story. Understanding what makes a character "tick" helps a reader know why a story unfolds the way it does. Below is a list of characters from the movie. Write down traits of each character and tell the effect you think those traits have on the story.

Bernie the Ogre

Trait	Effect on Story
_____	_____
	_____
_____	_____

Princess Stella

Trait	Effect on Story
_____	_____
	_____
_____	_____
	_____

Manco

Trait	Effect on Story
_____	_____
	_____

The Moles

Trait	Effect on Story
_____	_____
	_____

The Dragon

Trait	Effect on Story
_____	_____
	_____

D In the movie review "A Movie to Remember!", the reviewer is putting forth arguments to persuade the reader to go see the movie. It is his opinion that the movie is good. He uses a **slanted** argument to convince people that the movie is worth seeing.

Slanted arguments often use words with highly emotional meanings. These words may be **derogatory** ("negative words") or **laudatory** ("positive words"). On the line after each laudatory word taken from the review, write the opposite derogatory word from the box.

Derogatory Words

saddest	ugly
cruel	dishonest
common	annoying
undependable	depressing

Laudatory Words

1. funniest _____

2. extraordinary _____

3. picturesque _____

4. merciful _____

5. pleasant _____

6. responsible _____

7. truthful _____

8. upbeat _____

9. What are the four laudatory arguments that the reviewer lists to persuade the reader to see the movie about Bernie?

_____

_____

_____

_____

_____

An Historic Victory

In Spanish, the name *Cinco de Mayo* means the 5th of May. It is a Mexican holiday that all Americans should observe. The holiday celebrates an historic victory in the city of Puebla, Mexico, on May 5, 1862. Two groups of soldiers fought each other. A small Mexican army of soldiers and ordinary citizens battled against French forces. The French forces had better equipment and training, but the Mexican forces won the battle.

The Mexican army's victory was small. It did not end French control of Mexico. In fact, the French would conquer and rule Mexico for five more years. But the Battle of Puebla was important. It showed that ordinary Mexican citizens could fight against a powerful foreign force and win.

Why were French forces in Mexico? When the Battle of Puebla happened, Mexico was in trouble. The Mexican-American War had ended in 1848, and Mexico owed other countries a lot of money. The national treasury was almost empty. So in 1861, Mexican President Benito Juárez said that Mexico would not pay what it owed for two years. He promised to pay later, but France, Spain, and England did not want to wait. Each country sent people to collect the money Mexico owed them. In time, the Spanish and English worked out an agreement with President Juárez. They went back, but the French didn't.

Napoleon III of France wanted to take over Mexico and build a French empire. He made Maximilian the new ruler of his empire. He sent French troops to take control.

The French feared no one. They had not lost a single battle in 50 years. The French thought the Mexicans would give up without a fight, but they were wrong.

Texas-born General Ignacio Zaragoza waited for the French forces to come. He was ordered to defend the city of Puebla. The general had 2,000 troops and some loyal Puebla citizens. These poor people brought their farm tools to use as weapons.

The French soldiers charged the city. After only two hours, the battle ended. Many French soldiers had been killed or wounded. Despite the odds against them, the Mexican Army defeated the most powerful army in the world. Their victory strengthened the pride of the Mexican people. Their success on May 5, 1862, brought Mexicans together. They were determined to force the French out of their land.

The victory at the Battle of Puebla was also important for Americans. While the French moved toward Mexico City, the capital, President Juárez fled to northern Mexico. There he set up a temporary but powerful government to fight the French. The government's position in northern Mexico prevented the French army from getting supplies to Confederate rebels during the American Civil War. Mexican bravery gave the North another year to strengthen its military. In July 1863, little more than one year after the Battle of Puebla, Northern forces defeated the Confederates at the Battle of Gettysburg.

After the Civil War, President Lincoln told the French to get out of Mexico. He sent General Phil Sheridan and Union soldiers to the border between Texas and Mexico. There Sheridan gave Mexican troops the supplies they needed to control the French. In early 1867, Napoleon took his troops out of Mexico. The brave

Mexican people controlled their country again. Cinco de Mayo is not a celebration of Mexico's independence. It marks a day when Mexicans discovered how strong they are. Cinco de Mayo is a day that shows national pride. Today, many Mexican-Americans have parades and festivals on Cinco de Mayo. They play traditional music and dance. They share traditional food, arts, and crafts.

Some historians think other Americans should celebrate, too. If Mexico hadn't forced the French out of their country, the American Civil War might have ended differently. If the Confederates had won the war, the United States might be two countries instead of one. This is enough reason for Americans to celebrate Cinco de Mayo. There is also another good reason.

By recognizing Cinco de Mayo, Americans could learn more about people who showed great courage. They could appreciate what Americans owe those few, brave Mexican soldiers who fought in 1862.

Which holiday?

Holidays are important to different people for different reasons. What holiday is important in your family? Why? Write a brief explanation.

A **Underline the correct answer that completes each statement.**

1. The story about Cinco de Mayo is a
   a. compare and contrast article.
   b. biography.
   c. movie review.
   d. short report.

2. Cinco de Mayo celebrates
   a. the French victory over the Mexicans in the city of Puebla.
   b. the Mexican victory over the French in the city of Puebla.
   c. the North's victory over the South in the Civil War.
   d. the Mexican victory over the English in the city of Puebla.

3. The French were in Mexico because
   a. Benito Juarez invited the French to rule Mexico.
   b. the Mexican peasants wanted Maximilian to rule Mexico.
   c. General Zaragoza told Napoleon III that Mexico needed a ruler.
   d. Napoleon III wanted to take over Mexico and build a French empire.

4. The Mexican victory over the French was surprising because
   a. the Mexicans were outnumbered and were not as well equipped.
   b. there were fewer French troops than Mexican troops.
   c. the Mexicans were better trained and better equipped than the French.
   d. the French were not used to the Mexican countryside.

5. The Mexican victory at Puebla was important for the United States because
   a. it prevented Confederate troops from getting supplies from the French.
   b. it prevented Mexican troops from attacking the United States.
   c. it prevented the Union troops from getting supplies from the French.
   d. it prevented England from attacking the United States.

6. Cinco de Mayo marks a day that Mexicans discovered
   a. how weak they were.   b. how strong the Spanish were.
   c. how strong they were.   d. how weak the French were.

7. Cinco de Mayo is celebrated today with
   a. pumpkins and costumes.
   b. parades and festivals.
   c. hidden, decorated eggs.
   d. decorated trees and presents.

8. By learning about Cinco de Mayo, Americans could learn more about people
   a. in the Union army.   b. who showed great courage.
   c. who are English.   d. who like parades.

Read the list carefully. Then, follow the directions.

Possible Experts

the head of the Hispanic Studies department of the local college

the researcher at the local natural history museum

a neighbor who is interested in Mexican pottery

your history teacher at school

a friend who is taking Spanish

the head librarian at the local city library

the director of the Mexican culture section of the local art museum

1. Name the four experts you think might help you the most in finding out more about the history of Cinco de Mayo. List them in order, beginning with most knowledgeable.

    a. _____

    _____

    b. _____

    _____

    c. _____

    _____

    d. _____

    _____

2. What questions would you ask the experts?

    _____

    _____

    _____

    _____

    _____

    _____

    _____

The experts you picked have listened to your description. They make suggestions about research topics.

The experts suggested you look for:
- The history of Mexico and the city of Puebla
- Key people involved in the battle and politics at the time
- The Civil War
- French history around 1862
- Hispanic culture and festivals

You then go to the encyclopedia to look up information about the topics the experts mentioned. In which volumes should you look?

A-B	C-D	E-G	H-J	K-M	N-P	Q-R	S	T-V	W-Z
1	2	3	4	5	6	7	8	9	10

Think of at least eight specific topics you can look up. Write the information on the lines below. Use the headings given.

Volume	Letters	Topic
1. _____	_____	_____
2. _____	_____	_____
3. _____	_____	_____
4. _____	_____	_____
5. _____	_____	_____
6. _____	_____	_____
7. _____	_____	_____
8. _____	_____	_____

D One expert suggested that you use the Internet to further your research. There are programs on the Internet called search engines that can be a friendly guide for your research. A search engine sounds like some kind of machine, but it's really just another kind of web site—one that lets you search all the other web sites to find information about your topic. Type **key words** into the "search box" on the search engine page.

Key words are words that represent the subject you are looking for. For example, if you are in need of homework help, you might type the key words "homework+help" into the search box and then hit the search button next to it. This key word search will open a hot list of homework web sites that you can explore and choose from by clicking on each.

Back	Forward	Stop	Refresh	Home	AutoFill	Print	Mail

Address @ http://home.com

Search Engine ◆ | homework+help | Search

Think of a list of key words to type into a search engine that will lead you to more information about Cinco de Mayo.

Key Words	Topic
1. _____	_____
2. _____	_____
3. _____	_____
4. _____	_____
5. _____	_____
6. _____	_____
7. _____	_____
8. _____	_____
9. _____	_____
10. _____	_____

E **Factual** material can be proven true. The details can be checked in records or in the words of eyewitnesses.

Fictional material can be based on true facts. However, the author of fictional material might do some of the things listed in the box below. If any of these are present in shows, movies, plays, or writings, they are fictional materials.

> • put in impossible details that do not fit the time period
>
> • include impossible actions, events, or deeds
>
> • make up characters that do not exist but that act, talk, and dress as if they could
>
> • include conversations that no one can prove are the exact words spoken by the characters
>
> • contain characters such as ogres, giants, elves, witches, plants, animals, and people that are unheard of in real life

Below are parts of stories. The authors did not intend to write fiction. Some of the authors, however, changed factual material into fictional material based on fact. Label each story **fiction** or **fact.** If the story is fiction, underline the details that changed fact to fiction.

_____ 1. Have you heard about the Internet and wondered what it is all about? The Internet is about connections. Two computers that are connected, for example, can share information. This ability to share information makes the two computers a network. The Internet is a worldwide network of computers hooked up to one another. In fact, it is a system of millions of connected computer networks around the world.

_____ 2. These computer networks can take you almost any place on Earth. With the click of keys on a keyboard, you can plan a vacation, send an message to the other side of the world, or play a game with someone in Europe, all without leaving your chair.

_____ 3. When most people think of the Internet, they think of the Web. Web is short for the World Wide Web. But the Web and the Internet are different. The Internet is a system of computer networks and programs. It began in the early1960s. The Web was born thirty years later. It is a program that runs on the Internet. When you use your computer to connect to the Internet and then to the Web, you are online. Being online means you are using the Internet. The Web is made up of tiny robot spiders.

_____ 4. Besides a computer, you will need a little machine called a modem. A modem is a machine that connects your computer to a phone or cable TV line. The modem changes information from your computer into a form that can be carried along phone or cable lines. Then, the modem brings information back from the Internet into your computer, changing it into a form that your computer can understand. The modem might be in a box that sits on the desk next to your computer. A modem also might be a special card that fits inside your computer or your brain.

_____ 5. You will also need a phone or cable socket, or connector, to plug the modem into. Your modem doesn't need to be plugged into your phone line when you aren't using the Internet. But, it doesn't matter if you leave it plugged in. It won't stop you from receiving phone calls or being able to watch TV shows. But remember, when you are online, your phone line is in use, so you won't be able to get any calls, and no one will be able to use the phone.

_____ 6. A computer, a modem, and a phone or cable socket or connector are known as hardware. Hardware is the machinery you need to connect to the Internet.

_____ 7. To travel online, you also need software. Software is the name given to the programs that run on your computer. Some special software programs allow you to connect and see different places on the Internet and Web. So, before you can travel online, you need two things. First, you need an Internet Service Provider, or ISP. Second, you need a web browser. Third, you need a magic flying carpet.

F Rosa and Chita Garcia are going as exchange students to Mexico, a country in Central America. To plan their trip carefully, they will look up as much information as possible and speak to people who can help them. Follow the directions below.

1. Underline where they can go to find relevant information about the journey.
   a. a librarian
   b. a guard in a museum
   c. a Mexican artist
   d. a clerk at the airline office
   e. a travel agent
   f. an Internet Web site sponsored by the Mexican government
   g. a friend who lived in Mexico from 1999 to 2002

2. Circle the letters of four references that might give them the most relevant information.
   a. *Mexico's Neighbors*
   b. *Travel in Mexico on $50 a Day*
   c. *Atlas of Central America*
   d. *Recipes From Mexico*
   e. bus schedule of trips around Mexico
   f. *Travel to South America on $50 a Day*
   g. *Ancient Mexican Sights*

3. All these people have written books. Which three authors would most likely give the Garcias relevant information? Underline the answers.
   a. Jimmy Grant, a mechanic in South Texas, who services planes from Mexico
   b. Maria Cortez, the publicity agent of the Mexican Tourist Center
   c. Enrique Palmas, who wrote *Life of a Mexican Butterfly*
   d. Elena Cordoba, a writer who travels all over the world and reviews airplanes, hotels, and restaurants
   e. Sarah Goldberg, a geography professor, who writes for travel magazines

G **Choose a word from the box to complete each sentence.**

```
─────────────────── Word Box ───────────────────
    key words          technology          historic
    laughingstock      picturesque         fantastic
    search engine      unique              modem
    persuade           leprechaun          rescue
──────────────────────────────────────────────────
```

1. If something is one of a kind, it is _____.

2. A _____ spot is a very beautiful place.

3. The diver jumped into the pool to _____ the drowning man.

4. The raising of the United States flag on the moon was a very

   _____ occasion.

5. The new computer _____ allows for links into satellite broadcasts.

6. The commercial tried to _____ the audience to buy the toothpaste.

7. A very wild tale is called a _____ story.

8. She typed _____ into the search engine window in order to find information to complete her research.

9. The _____ escaped to protect his pot of gold.

10. The other ogres made fun of Bernie, making him feel like a

    _____.

11. A _____ is a little machine that connects a computer to a phone or a cable TV line.

12. A _____ is a Web page that allows a user to look for information on the Internet by typing in key words.

Read the article below. The author is trying to convince you to take a speech class. Underline the persuasive argument(s) in each paragraph.

Take a Speech Class!

What happened the last time you stood up to speak to your class? Did your knees shake so hard that your teacher went to the door to see who was knocking? Did your voice wobble so much that you sounded like a child's toy? Did sweat roll from under your arms down your sides and plop to the floor? Did your eyes blink so often you thought someone had turned off the lights? If your answer to any of these important questions is yes, then you should take a speech class.

There are so many good reasons for taking a speech class that it's hard to decide where to begin. But I'll try anyway. Taking a speech class makes you confident. What does it mean to be confident? For one thing, it means you can stand up to talk without shaking like the last leaf on a tree in a heavy windstorm. It means you can speak in a language that sounds like English. It also means your classmates won't roll their eyes while you're talking. They'll be listening. And they'll listen because you sound like you know what you're talking about.

So, how do you make this happen? In a speech class, you'll learn to think before you speak. No doubt, you've heard that one before. But in this case, it's good advice. Here's why. You can't talk about something you don't know anything about. Well, I guess you could, but there go your classmates' eyes again. People can tell when the person who's talking to them doesn't know what he or she is talking about. They can also tell when someone isn't prepared to speak. You've probably noticed that yourself. How long does a speaker like that keep your attention? Not long.

Thinking before speaking can make you confident, and this is what you will practice in a speech class. Let's say, for example, that on the first day of school, your teacher gives you a homework assignment. You must come to school the next day ready to tell the class how you spent your summer vacation.

The night before class, you could decide to "wing it." Basically, that means you don't think about the assignment at all. You think the most important thing you can do to prepare is to show up for class. Well, we know what happens when you do that. Speech class will teach you how to prepare and rehearse a speech.

This time, sit down and take out some paper. Make a list of everything you did over the summer. If the list says only summer school, you have a problem. Your speech could be a disaster unless you add a little spice. I don't mean lie. I mean think harder! Speech class will help you learn about adding zip and spice by having you ask yourself questions. What happened in summer school? Whom did you meet? What special projects did you do? Whom did you sit with at lunchtime? Name two things you did that were outstanding. Do you understand where I'm going here?

Okay. Now that your list covers both sides of your paper, you're ready. Go through the list and choose one or two things you really want to talk about. Learning about what not to talk about is just as important as learning about what to talk about; you will learn this with practice in class. Now, get out a new piece of paper.

Don't write every detail. Speech class teaches that relating a few main ideas well will capture your audience's attention. Go for the main ideas. List them in the order you want to talk about them. Then use a few words or phrases that will help you remember what you want to say about each main idea. When you reach the end, move to a mirror. That's right. Move to a mirror. Look yourself straight in the eye and start talking! Say everything you want to say to the class, and say it over and over again. Say it so often that you can remember what you want to say without using the piece of paper in your hands.

The big moment comes. It's your turn to talk. You've practiced your speech. You know what you want to say. The problem is that the people out there don't look like the person in the mirror. But they are. They're just like you, only less prepared. Breathe deeply. Look at the crowd. Be brave. Move forward. This probably won't be the best speech you'll ever give, but it's a start. And after you finish speech class, no one will ever hear your knees knock again.

B **Read the ads below. Put a ✓ beside the ads that give you the factual information you need to know about a product.**

_____ 1. The new E-track Computer helps you keep track of all the details in your life. It has an html database built in that will manage your address book, your class schedule, and all your calendar needs. The E-track also has a GPS, global positioning satellite feature, that lets you connect with an interactive map. You will never be lost again!

_____ 2. The Magic Genie Cleanser will remove any stain. As our spokesperson, beautiful actress Monica Moore, says—"There's no spot the Genie can't handle . . . try it today!"

_____ 3. Candidate Bob Hoskins says, "A vote for me is a vote for you!" Recommended by thinking people everywhere! Remember to vote for Bob on November 12!

_____ 4. Crunchies Cereal is the healthiest cereal on the market. It contains the daily requirements set by the Food and Drug Administration for protein content; calcium; niacin; and vitamins C, D, and E.

C **Read the story below. Then, answer the questions about character, mood, and setting.**

"*Qué pasa*, Mama?" I asked softly.

Mama wiped her hands on her flowered apron and sat down, looking at me sadly. I had never seen my mama sit down during the day. She was always cooking, cleaning, or washing something. But now she sat. I knew it must be bad news. I listened as she began to speak.

"You know we love you, *cariño*?"

"*Claro que sí*," I answered. " Of course, yes." I squirmed in my seat holding my breath, waiting for the heavy blow to fall.

"Your papa has lost his job, Maria. We are sending you to live with your *abuelita* until he can find another." Mama smiled a small, sad smile. "It will be fine. You'll see." There were tears in her pleading eyes.

"No. No. No!" I shouted at her, running out of the *casa*.

I ran and ran. I ran past my friends playing in the long, silvery grasses of the vacant lot. I passed them silently like a misty ghost.

"*Hola*, Maria, where are you going?" they yelled out, their voices echoing in the greyness of the overcast morning.

I ran down the dusty road that led to the village, searching for some quiet. But the wind roared in my ears and blew my tears down my neck and into my collar. My heart beat so loudly, I could hear it, too.

I ran into the village. The noisy, jangling market was just opening. Someone laughed and their laughter stung me. A nice, smiling woman handed me a cup of *arroz con dulce*. I tried to smile my thanks, but my face felt frozen. I put a spoonful of the sweet pudding into my mouth. I could not swallow. The rest of my tears and the pudding seemed to stick like thick clay in my throat.

1. What word would you use to describe Maria?
   a. happy   b. shocked
   c. hysterical   d. friendly

2. What word would you use to describe Maria's mother?
   a. angry   b. abrupt
   c. pleading   d. talkative

3. What color would you use to describe the mood of the story?
   a. yellow   b. pink
   c. purple   d. grey

4. List some descriptive words that set the mood of the story.

D Your art teacher has assigned you a painting to study at the local art museum. It is by the French impressionist painter Claude Monet and was painted in 1880. Answer the questions below about how to proceed in your research.

1. Underline the relevant references you might use.

   a. *Great Masterpieces of France in the 19th Century*

   b. *European Art and Artists*

   c. a magazine about collage

   d. *Art in America*

   e. *The Best of French Artists: 1600–1800*

   f. *Children of Famous Painters*

   g. *A Guide to European Painters*

2. Circle the letters of experts you might consult.

   a. your art teacher

   b. a friend who is taking painting lessons

   c. the director of the city art museum

   d. the man who runs the local art supply shop

   e. the head librarian in the art library

   f. a neighbor who collects art

   g. a man in the paint section at the local mall department store

3. All these people have written books. Which three authors would most likely give you relevant information? Underline the answers.

   a. Emile Dubois, *German Abstract Art in the 1800s*

   b. Mary Goodfellow, the editor of the *Art Digest*

   c. Jeff Romero, who wrote *A Look at the Impressionists*

   d. Tanisha Wright, *How to Paint Your Kitchen*

   e. Mai Wong, *From Albers to Zola: A Look at Great Artists and Their Patrons*

4. Circle the letters of key words that you might type into an Internet search engine.

   a. expressionism

   b. French+artists

   c. impressionism

   d. Monet

   e. ancient+art

E Read the following fairy stories. What facts of nature were early people trying to explain? Write the correct fact of nature under each myth.

```
┌──────── Facts of Nature ────────┐
│  lightning and thunder          │
│  why volcanoes erupt            │
│  what rainbows are              │
│  the seasons of the year        │
└─────────────────────────────────┘
```

1.   There is a Chinese story that tells about a magic fish. The fish, when seen leaping out of the water in an arc, brings good luck to the observer. The scales of the fish are many colors: red, orange, blue, green, gold. What do you think this explains?

_____

2.   In South America there is a legend about a powerful being who lives inside a mountain. When the being is happy, he is very quiet and only the sound of the wind can be heard. But, when he is unhappy, he throws rocks and hot mud from the top of his home among the clouds. What do you think this explains?

_____

3.   In Africa there is a story about a great lion whose roar shakes the earth. His golden eyes and mane shoot tremendous sparks. The lion brings rain to the dry plains. What do you think this explains?

_____

Answer Key

Story 1
pages 5–11

A 1. c 5. b
2. a 6. d
3. b 7. b
4. a 8. d

B Answers may vary. Possible answer: The writer feels badly because she cannot swim. Her older cousin, J.W., makes fun of her. The writer watches her cousin, Danny, and sees his courage. Her brother, Donnie, offers swim lessons and she accepts. Everyone is proud of her at the end for learning to swim. The lessons in the story are to act in the face of teasing, learn from the courage of others, and ask for or accept help.

C 1. shallow 9. rapids
2. conceited 10. dunking
3. panicked 11. enthusiastic
4. reunions 12. basked
5. compliment 13. embarrassment
6. shriveled 14. squishing
7. imitating 15. agony
8. initiation

D 1. J.W. is a hurtful teaser.
2. We know more about the world, so it seems smaller.
3. Principal Jones is asking for help with the physical labor.
4. Sarah would do anything for a friend, even walk a mile.
5. Karim didn't fit in at school.
6. The hikers slept deeply and didn't move.

Story 2
pages 12–22

A 1. d 5. b
2. d 6. d
3. b 7. a
4. c 8. c

B 1. highway—red, yellow
2. trees—live oaks, cottonwoods
3. years—40
4. former owner—agent
5. box—pocketknife
6. overnight bag—Cole stays at his dad's on weekends. This is a clue that his parents are separated or divorced.

C 1. a. Detail
   b. Main Idea
   c. Detail
2. a. Detail
   b. Detail
   c. Detail
   d. Main Idea
3. a. Main Idea
   b. Detail
   c. Detail
   d. Detail
4. a. Detail
   b. Main Idea
   c. Detail
5. a. Detail
   b. Main Idea
   c. Detail
   d. Detail

D 1. Cody might want to use the library to find out about the Medal of Honor; he might want to use the Internet to look up a Medal of Honor site; he may want to write to a branch of the military.
2.–4. Cody should probably look through the house first to find out other information; he might visit the local courthouse or county website; he might want to interview older neighbors to see if they remember Horace; Cody could use the Internet to find out what branch of the service Horace was in and more about why his medal was awarded to him.

E Answers will vary. Story chart should include some of the research steps given in Activity D and the prediction about who Horace Mickel is. The chart should provide a beginning, a middle, and an end.

F 1855, 1861, 1863, 1864, 1865, 1866, 1919

1855 Mary Walker becomes a doctor.

1861 Cares for wounded from the Battle of Bull Run.

1863 Serves close to battlefield.

1864 Captured by Confederates, then released.

1865 Awarded medal.

1866 Speaks out for women's right to vote.

1919 Dies. Nineteenth Amendment is passed.

Story 3
pages 23–31

A 1. b   4. a
    2. b   5. d
    3. c   6. a

B 1. Ameila Jones Locker and James Locker, Jr.
    2. James Locker, Sr.
    3. Johnny Locker
    4. Lucy Riley Locker
    5. no
    6. Ralph Jones and James Locker
    7. Tamisha Marie Jones, her grandmother

C 1. cheerful—depressed
    2. overdue—on time
    3. serious—humorous
    4. forget—remember
    5. tightening—stretching
    6. amazing—ordinary
    7. secret—open
    8. unashamed—embarrassed
    9. disappeared—showed
    10. talked out of—convinced

D 1. bashful
    2. predict
    3. attach
    4. air freshener
    5. siblings
    6. persist
    7. highlight
    8. industrious
    9. reality
    10. balanced

E 1. 4 P.M.
    2. Bus students
    3. a pass from the principal, a note from parents or guardians, a list of math questions
    4. sign-up sheet
    5. a list of math questions
    6. 8 A.M.
    7. Sierra Room in the library
    8. So they have a good, quiet atmosphere for studying and reading.

F 1. O   9. O
    2. F   10. F
    3. F   11. F
    4. O   12. F
    5. F   13. O
    6. F   14. F
    7. O   15. O
    8. F

Story 4
pages 32–40

A 1. b   5. d
    2. b   6. b
    3. a   7. d
    4. c

B 1. North America
    2. United States
    3. Louisiana
    4. Swampy, hot and humid, with wildlife like muskrats and alligators
    5. Cajun land, jambalaya country

C 1. true   7. true
    2. false   8. true
    3. true   9. true
    4. false   10. true
    5. false   11. true
    6. false   12. false

D 1. M   6. M
    2. M   7. S
    3. S   8. S
    4. M   9. M
    5. S   10. S

E Answers may vary depending on dictionary used.

    1. Acadian French—a native of Louisiana
    2. Carib or Arawak Indian—a dugout canoe
    3. French—a fried square doughnut
    4. American French—a spicy stew
    5. Taino or Carib Indian—a fire pit with wood for cooking
    6. Latin and Greek—a change of form
    7. Latin—a time of celebration
    8. Latin and Greek—a figure of speech that includes an inferred comparison
    9. French—U.S. state on the Gulf of Mexico named for Louis XIV of France

Story 5
pages 41–47

A 1. c   5. c
    2. c   6. b
    3. b   7. d
    4. a

B 1, 5, 3, 7, 2, 9, 4, 6, 8

C 1. blackened—darkened
    2. veteran—experienced
    3. reject—discard
    4. show—demonstrate
    5. cradle—hold

6. emerge—come out of

7. continue—sustain

8. take part in—participate

9. industrious—hardworking

10. rebellion—protest

11. theory—idea

D
1. apparatus
2. flora
3. specimen
4. species
5. principle
6. catalog
7. kinetic energy
8. dowel
9. cargo
10. demonstrate

E
1. h
2. e
3. a
4. g
5. b
6. f
7. i
8. c
9. d

Skills Review (Stories 1–5) pages 48–54

A Underline:

Paragraph 1: But, chameleons live in many different habitats all over the continent of Africa and on the island country of Madagascar just off the coast of Africa.

Paragraph 2: The rain forest is ideal for chameleons.

Paragraph 3: Chameleons are reptiles, or cold-blooded crawling animals.

Paragraph 4: Chameleons are also lizards, but they differ from other lizards in a few ways.

Paragraph 5: Chameleons have bulging, heavy-lidded eyes that have are unique.

Paragraph 6: This special color-changing feature makes chameleons of interest to scientists.

1. This special color-changing feature makes chameleons of interest to scientists.
2. b
3. d
4. a
5. e
6. Student answers may vary, but might include: Chameleon's skin can change color with changes in light, temperature, and mood; scientists might be interested in finding out what causes this change genetically; this color change might have medical or military uses.

B Underline Opinions:

Paragraph 1: It is sad that such an advanced culture is no more.

Paragraph 2: Perhaps the Maya were looking for some peace after all their troubles.

Paragraph 3: Gold is difficult for everyone to resist since it is so beautiful.

Paragraph 4: Maybe the Spanish did not care for the Mayan art style.

Summary:

The Mayan civilization began to weaken around A.D. 900. They began to leave their cities and customs. To escape enemies, they moved their capital to a walled city called Mayapan. When the Spanish came for gold, they began to slowly conquer the Maya. By 1697 all Maya were under the Spanish until 1821 when Mexico won its independence.

C
Paragraph 1—b
Paragraph 2—e
Paragraph 3—c
Paragraph 4—a

D 300, 638, 700, 800–900, 980, 1502,1546, 1697, 1821

300—A Mayan royal ruling class develops.

638—The great king of the Maya, Pascal, dies.

700—Mayan culture is at its height.

800–900—The Maya begin to leave their cities.

980—The Toltecs conquer the Maya.

1502—Columbus meets Mayan traders.

1546—The Spanish conquer the Yucatan Maya.

1697—The last Maya city is defeated by the Spanish.

1821—Mexico wins independence from Spain.

E
1. ferocious, mild
2. resist, join
3. theory, fact
4. condense, lengthen
5. camouflaged, exposed
6. regulated, uncontrolled
7. enlist, resign
8. release, seize
9. actual, fantasy
10. tore down, upheld
11. invite, repulse

F
1. catalog, list
2. irrigated, watered
3. conquered, took over
4. succession, in line
5. specific, detailed
6. peninsula, finger of land
7. moist, damp
8. temperate, mild
9. siege, battle
10. society, civilization
11. potential, power

G 1. b
   2. a
   3. a
   4. c

Story 6
pages 55–63

A 1. c   6. b
   2. b   7. c
   3. d   8. d
   4. a
   5. d

B In-line Skates and Ice Skates
I.
  A.
    2. Both let a skater skate well all the time.
    3. Both can be used in more than one sport.
  B.
    1. Both have boots that help support the ankles.
II.
  A.
    2. In-line skates have a plastic boot. Ice skates have a leather boot.
    3. In-line skates have a removable, washable liner. Ice skates do not have a liner.
  B.
    1. In-line skates have wheels.
    2. Ice skates have blades.
  C.
    1. In-line skates have brakes.
    2. Ice skates do not have brakes.

C 1. b
   2. d
   3. b
   4. d
   5. Ice skating is an older sport and has skaters of all ages; people in colder U.S. climates learn to ice skate on local ponds and lakes when they are young.

D 1. ice skating
   2. in-line skating
   3. The comparisons all indicate that the weather is cold, winter weather. The cold "bites my face," "splintering air," and "crisp blue sky."
   4. She says her wheels "'whine. . . singing and clicking" like the noises a dolphin makes.
   5. Heat waves bouncing off of shiny objects makes the atmosphere look like it shimmers and shifts.

E 1. plastic   6. mileage
   2. splintering   7. perspiration
   3. limber   8. embarrassment
   4. sports   9. paper
   5. skate wheels

F 1. The measurement was <u>approximate</u>, but not exact.
   2. Because she is <u>ambitious</u>, she wants to make the Honor's List.
   3. The green leaves fell in the pond water and began to <u>deteriorate</u>.
   4. He had missed out on the <u>fundamentals</u> of algebra and was behind in the class.
   5. She is a dancer and is very <u>limber</u>.

G 1. tireless   5. strenuous
   2. spirited   6. unfailing
   3. lively   7. strong
   4. energetic   8. unweary

Story 7
pages 64–72

A 1. c   5. d
   2. a   6. a
   3. c   7. b
   4. b   8. d

B A History of Spices
I.
  B. Pepper
    1. Grows on shrubs as a berry
  C.
    1. From the female parts of the purple saffron crocus flower
    2. Yellow-orange powder
    3. Slender red threads
II.
  A.
    1. Seasoning
    2. Preserving food
    3. Medicine
    4. Preserving bodies
    5. Pay and coins
  B.
    1. Gifts for royalty
    2. Medicine for heart and kidneys
  C. Saffron
    1. Seasoning
    2. Medicine
    3. Honor guests
    4. Dye cloth
    5. Perfume
    6. Dye hair
    7. Sign of wealth and power
III.
  A.
  B. Romans in India
  C.
  D. Portugese
  E. British
    1. Queen Elizabeth I involved in India in 1600s
    2. British East India Company
    3. Control in 18th Century

IV.
A. British tax on salt in India
B. Mohandas Ghandi march to sea to protest
C. British withdrew from India in 1947

C 1. Indonesia
2. sovereign
3. nonviolent
4. evaporates
5. seasonings
6. preserve
7. spectator
8. blockade

D **Across**   **Down**
1. sal dare   2. dryers
3. pepper   5. blockades
4. shrub   7. unless
6. opens   9. trial
8. skate
10. lesson
11. daisies
12. salt

E Time Line

3,000 B.C.	Chinese write about salt as medicine.
mid-300s B.C.	Greeks conquer southern Asia.
27 B.C.	People in Egypt and Rome use salt as a cloth dye.
A.D. 408	Hippocrates uses pepper as medicine.
A.D. 600s	Arabs conquer India.
1498	Vasco da Gama challenges Arabs in India.
mid-1500s	Court of Henry VIII uses saffron as a hair dye.
1600s	Queen Elizabeth I sends traders to India.
1700s (18th c.)	British secure spice trade.
1947	India wins independence from Britain.

Story 8
pages 73–82

A 1. b   5. b
2. c   6. c
3. d   7. b
4. a   8. c

B Summaries may vary. Example:
Barbara French takes care of bats that have been injured and have to live in captivity. One December day Barbara's bats began acting strangely. One of the males, Hank, was singing like a bird. Bats that had always liked to snuggle up to each other and roost together were suddenly fighting. Barbara was anxious about these changes, so she asked Amanda Lollar, an expert in the care of captive Mexican free-tailed bats, what was happening. Barbara learned that the singing and fighting were mating behaviors. These behaviors stopped once the female bats started having pups. Both Barbara and scientists who study bats learned quite a lot about the mating behaviors of Mexican free-tailed bats from this experience.

C Answers may vary.
Paragraph 1: SD,SR, M, SD, SD, SD, SD, SR, SR
Paragraph 2: M, SD, SD, SD, SD, SR
Paragraph 3: SD, M, SD, SD
Paragraph 4: SD, M, SD
Paragraph 5: SR, M, SD, SD, SD, SD, SR
Paragraph 6: SD, M, SD
Paragraph 7: SD, M, SD, SD, SD, SD
Paragraph 8: M, SD, SD, SD, SD, SD, SD, SD, SD
Paragraph 9: SD, SD, SR, M, SD

D 1. pollinators
2. roosting
3. compete
4. echolocation
5. membrane
6. nocturnal
7. fertilizer
8. excursion
9. squabble
10. environment

Four Positive Things That Bats Do
Bats are <u>insectivores</u> and keep the insect population in check.
Bats are <u>pollinators</u> and increase crop production.
Undigested seeds in bat <u>guano</u> grow new plants, like fruit trees.
Bat <u>guano</u> makes excellent <u>fertilizer</u>.

E 1. Hypothesis: The temperature has risen above freezing, causing melting. Proof: Put a temperature gauge, or thermometer, outside to see if the temperature has risen above 32 degrees F.
2. Hypothesis: An earthquake is happening. Proof: After the shaking stops, check the news stations for reports of a quake.
3. Hypothesis: My frog is not as good a jumper as my friend's frog. Proof: Repeat the experiment by holding a series of jumping tests. If my frog continues to be slow, I know my hypothesis is correct.

F Likenesses and Differences

Likenesses: Both have ears that are set on the head; both can hear between 2 decibels and 20 decibels; both have like structures—tympanum, eustachian tube, anvil.

Differences: Ear of bat sits up high on head like an antenna; human ear fits close and low on head; bat ear receives sound at higher levels, from 20 to 40 decibels; the structures on bat ear are more complex, larger, flatter, shorter eustachian tube.

Story 9
pages 83–88

A 1. c   5. a
     2. d   6. b
     3. b   7. d
     4. d   8. a

B 1. Practicing good manners on the Internet.
     2. Practice netiquette so people will want to talk to you and so you won't be banned from the Internet by the ISP.
     3. An ISP provides the electronic link between the computer and the Internet.
     4. Typing in capital letters means you are shouting.
     5. Flaming means to type angrily. Harassing someone is bothering them.

C 1. b   5. a
     2. a   6. b
     3. b   7. a
     4. a   8. b

Skills Review
(Stories 6–9)
pages 89–96

A Underline.

Paragraph 1: <u>India is more crowded than almost anywhere else on Earth.</u>

Paragraph 2: <u>It is also called a subcontinent.</u>

Paragraph 3: <u>Politically and geographically, India is in a very important location.</u>

Paragraph 4: <u>India is a country of contrasts, and some people have described it as the "country that is many countries."</u>

Paragraph 5: <u>Ancient beliefs echo from the past into modern India.</u>

Paragraph 6: <u>The early phase of Asian-Indian movement, or migration, began around 1900 and lasted only until 1917.</u>

Paragraph 7: <u>The later phase of migration began after 1965, when the Immigration Act was passed.</u>

B 1. d   5. b
     2. a   6. d
     3. b   7. c
     4. c   8. a

C India and Immigration

I.
  A.
     1. Second largest population
     2. Seventh largest area
     3. A subcontinent
     4. Part of southern Asia

  B.
     1. Juts into Indian Ocean
     2. Himalaya Mountains in North
     3. Nepal, China, Tibet in North
     4. Pakistan on Northwest
     5. Bangladesh and Myanmar to East
  C.
     1. Mix of people from attacks, invasions, migrations
     2. Over 200 languages
     3. Hindi is the main language
II.
  A.
     1. priests
     2. princes
     3. businesspeople and farmers
     4. workers
     5. untouchables
  B.
     1. Hindus
     2. Muslims
     3. Sikhs
     4. Christians
     5. Buddhists
     6. Jains
III.
  A.
     1. six or seven thousand men
     2. went to California for adventure, jobs, and freedom
     3. came from rural areas
     4. were mainly uneducated
  B.
     1. from all over India
     2. higher educational levels
     3.
       a. Los Angeles, CA
       b. New York, NY
       c. Independence Town, NJ
       d. Houston, TX

D 1. immigrants   6. sewer
     2. traditions   7. Hindi
     3. caste   8. migration
     4. priests   9. contrasts
     5. census   10. invasions

E 1. c   3. d
     2. b   4. d

F 1. b   9. b
     2. a   10. a
     3. a   11. b
     4. b   12. a
     5. b   13. a
     6. a   14. a
     7. a   15. b
     8. b   16. b

Story 10
pages 97–103

A
1. c
2. d
3. c
4. a
5. a
6. b
7. d
8. c

B
1. what rainbows were
2. what thunder was
3. how two mountain ranges formed

C Character Traits and Effects
Bernie/1. Trait: Ticklish. Effect: Mole whiskers might tickle Bernie and anger dragon. 2. Trait: Bernie wants to be like other ogres; afraid of being laughingstock. Effect: Might make him try to avoid moles and moles' whiskers, including Stella. Princess Stella/1. Trait: Is a mole. Effect: Might tickle Bernie. 2. Trait: Strong, likes to laugh. Effect: Might influence Bernie to not care what other ogres think about him. 3. Trait: Responsible, cares about village. Effect: Stella will probably defy dragon and try to escape. Manco/1. Trait: Never smiles, likes to see others unhappy. Effect: Will probably try to keep Bernie from saving Princess Stella. The Moles/1. Trait: Courageous and persistent. Effect: Will not leave Bernie alone until he helps Stella. Dragon/1. Trait: Laughter makes him fire-breathing mad. Effect: Bernie's and Stella's laughter might make him so mad, he burns up his own castle.

D
1. saddest
2. common
3. ugly
4. cruel
5. annoying
6. undependable
7. dishonest
8. depressing
9. Arguments used by reviewer: Funniest fairy-tale ever; Interesting characters; Full of surprises; Unique, amazing computer graphics; Different from other fairy tales

Story 11
pages 104–114

A
1. d
2. b
3. d
4. a
5. a
6. c
7. b
8. b

B
1. Order of Experts
   a. the head of the Hispanic Studies department at the local college
   b. the director of the Mexican culture section of the local art museum
   c. your history teacher at school
   d. the head librarian at the local city library

2. Questions will vary.

C Answers will vary. Any topic relating to Cinco de Mayo is acceptable.

D Answers will vary. Any list of key words and topics related to Cinco de Mayo is acceptable.

E
1. fact
2. fact
3. fiction
4. fiction
5. fact
6. fact
7. fiction

F
1. a, d, e, f, g
2. b, c, e, g
3. b, d, e

G
1. unique
2. picturesque
3. rescue
4. historic
5. technology
6. persuade
7. fantastic
8. key words
9. leprechaun
10. laughingstock
11. modem
12. search engine

Skills Review
(Stories 10–11)
pages 115–119

A
1. If your answer to any of these important questions is yes, then you should take a speech class.
2. There are so many good reasons to take a speech class that it's hard to know where to begin. Taking a speech class makes you confident.
3. In a speech class, you'll learn to think before you speak.
4. Thinking before speaking can make you confident, and this is what you will practice in a speech class.
5. Speech class will teach you how to prepare and rehearse a speech.
6. Speech class will help you learn about adding zip and spice by having you ask yourself questions.
7. Learning about what not to talk about is just as important as learning about what to talk about; you will learn this with practice.
8. Speech class teaches that relating a few main ideas well will capture your audience's attention.
9. After you finish speech class, no one will ever hear your knees knock again.

B Check ✔ 1 and ✔ 4.

C
1. b
2. c
3. d
4. heavy, silvery, silently, misty ghost, greyness of the overcast morning, frozen, thick clay

D
1. Underline a, b, g
2. Circle a, c, e, f
3. Underline b, c, e
4. Circle b, c, d

E
1. what rainbows are
2. why volcanoes erupt
3. lightning and thunder